William Ritchie Sorley

Jewish Christians and Judaism

A study in the history of the first two centuries

William Ritchie Sorley

Jewish Christians and Judaism
A study in the history of the first two centuries

ISBN/EAN: 9783337246945

Printed in Europe, USA, Canada, Australia, Japan

Cover: Foto ©Lupo / pixelio.de

More available books at **www.hansebooks.com**

JEWISH CHRISTIANS
AND JUDAISM

A STUDY IN THE HISTORY OF THE FIRST TWO CENTURIES

BY

W. R. SORLEY

SCHOLAR OF TRINITY COLLEGE, CAMBRIDGE
SHAW FELLOW OF THE UNIVERSITY OF EDINBURGH

CAMBRIDGE
DEIGHTON BELL AND CO.
LONDON: GEORGE BELL AND SONS
1881

THE Hulsean Dissertation for 1880, which is now published, is an attempt to trace the relation which the Jewish Christians of the first two centuries bore to Judaism. Without pretending to be an exhaustive discussion, it seeks to point out the way in which the new faith was distinguished from the old, and to follow the successive steps by which this difference became manifest. In one aspect it may be regarded as a criticism of the Tübingen theory. But its aim is rather to give an independent view of a distinct, though related, subject. The limits of an historical essay have been closely adhered to throughout; and the conclusions arrived at have been made to depend, as little as possible, on the decision of questions in dispute amongst literary critics.

W. R. S.

CONTENTS.

	PAGE
I. Introductory: nature of the subject and its relation to the Tübingen theory	1
II. State of Judaism at the time when Christianity arose	5
1. Want of national homogeneity: Hebrews and Hellenists .	5
2. Want of religious harmony: Pharisees, Sadducees, and Essenes, and their relation to Christianity	7
III. Relation of Jewish Christians to Judaism in the Apostolic Age	14
A. Preparatory:	
1. Meaning of the term 'Jewish Christian'	14
2. Review of Authorities .	17
B. The three stages of this relationship . . .	24
1. The Belief in the Messiahship of Jesus as differentiating the early Christians from other Jews .	25
(1) The implications of this belief seen chiefly from its place in the writings of the Apostles .	28
(2) Its immediate result distinguishing Christians from Jews	31
(a) missionary character of Christianity	31
(b) persecution of Christians by the Jews .	31
(c) independent organization of the Christians .	32

			PAGE
	2. Traditional external observances still adhered to		33
	3. The Conflict between the new idea and these external customs		34
	(1) Origin of the conflict .		35
	(2) The conflict itself		36
	(a) The Council of Jerusalem, its parties, and the decision		37
	(b) The Schism at Antioch: its real significance		40
	(3) The result of the conflict . . .		43
	Consequent attitude of Christianity to Judaism . .		44
C.	State of Parties at the close of the Apostolic Age . .		48
	1. The Paulinists, now quite freed from Judaism .		48
	2. The older apostles (who seem to have kept the law without regarding its observance as essential) .		49
	3. The extreme 'Jewish Christians' or 'Judaizers' .		50
IV. The Post-Apostolic Age			52
distinguished from the preceding chiefly by one external event, the destruction of the Temple			52
A. Effect of this event,			
	1. On the Jews		52
	2. On the Christians		55
	(1) narrower effect on those in Palestine . .		55
	(2) more catholic effect on the thought of the Church		56
B. Authorities for this part of the subject . . .			57
C. The consequent relation of the Jewish Christians to Judaism.			
Difference between their external and their doctrinal relation			58
	1. The external relation . . .		59
	(1) Traces of original unseparatedness (?)		59
	(2) Explicit break from the side of Judaism . .		61
	(3) Consequences of this		63

CONTENTS. vii

	PAGE
2. The theological or doctrinal relation	65
(1) Position as to legal observance	66
(2) Position as to Christology	69
(a) attitude of the Jews to the Jewish Christians	69
(α) first attitude: abstract monotheism	70
(β) modified position: nomism	71
(b) attitude of the Jewish Christians	73
(3) Resultant Jewish Christian sects in their mutual relation and relation to Judaism	74
(a) Nazarenes and Ebionites	74
(b) Essene Christians: their relation to the Essenes	80
(α) in custom	80
(β) in doctrine	81
(γ) their identification	83
V. Review and Conclusion	84

I PURPOSE in the following pages to discuss a question closely connected with, but yet distinct from, the main theory of the Tübingen school. This theory, which is chiefly associated with the name of Ferdinand Christian Baur, aims at a reconstruction of the history of early Christianity, and of the purpose and origin of the Christian Scriptures, based on a thorough-going distinction between Jewish and Gentile Christians. Baur holds that this difference was far more deeply rooted and extensive than previous historians had imagined or the Christian records would have us believe. Founding his argument on the admitted dissensions in the early Church, borne witness to by the Epistles of St Paul—especially the Epistle to the Galatians and the First Epistle to the Corinthians—and by the Acts of the Apostles, he contends that in the latter work there is a systematic attempt to gloss over the depth of difference between the two parties and to narrow the extent of their quarrels—an attempt which bears the impress of a time when the opponents were (through the influence of the persecutions that pressed on them from without) coming to terms, and might be brought still closer by a historian who could so judiciously blend fact and fiction as to cool the heated memory of former strife and to make believe that the contending parties had from the outset been very much at one.

This mediating tendency it is which Baur thinks he has succeeded in exposing. He contends that the difference between Jewish and Gentile Christians was one not of race or social custom merely, but in their fundamental conceptions of Christianity, and that the former had much more in common with the unbelieving Jews than with the Gentile converts of Paul and his Hellenistic fellow-workers. As Zeller puts it in his essay on the Tübingen school[1], "Baur took his stand on the fact that the apostles and the apostolic age were already divided by the opposition of Judaism and Paulinism, of a particularistic and a universalistic, an Old Testament legal and a freer conception of Christianity, that this opposition died out only gradually after many contests and attempts at reconciliation, and that it first reached its term in the second half of the second century in the Catholic Church and its dogmatic. In that deep-reaching opposition Baur sees the impelling force by which the development of the Church proceeded for more than a century; by the position they adopted towards it the dogmatic character of individuals and parties are, according to him, determined; the monuments of the conflicts and mediations by which it was brought to an end we still have in the extra-canonical and in the New Testament writings. Every stage of the way which the Church left behind it in its development is marked by writings some of which are (for the most part incorrectly) ascribed to the apostles or to pupils of the apostles, and, in the sequel, were placed along-

---

[1] *Vorträge und Abhandlungen* (1865), p. 287.

side of the sacred codex of the Jews as a New Testament collection."

The object of the remarkable series of works inaugurated by the article on 'The Christ-party in the Corinthian Church[1]' is to trace the relation of the Jewish Christians to their Gentile brethren. But the historical picture painted there has also its obverse side—that of their relation to Judaism and the Jews; and it is to this aspect of the question that the present dissertation seeks to draw attention.

Not only are these two sides of the question closely bound together, but perhaps it is not too much to say that the latter aspect, though it has received less attention than the former, is really the more fundamental of the two. We can scarcely take a single step with Baur in tracing the successive conflicts and reconciliations between the Paulinist and the Petrinist, the Gentile and the Jewish Christian parties, without being driven back to consider the relation in which the Jewish or Petrinist party stood to the traditional doctrines and customary observances of Judaism. The sharp distinctions which Baur seeks to make out between the two parties in the Church are, at the same time, an argument for the closer connection of one of these parties with the hereditary worship and creed. The more the Jewish Christians are separated from the Paulinists the nearer are they brought to the non-Christian Jews. Every characteristic which is made to distinguish them from the former is equally and at the same time a bond uniting them to the latter.

And just in the same way we cannot go along with the opponents of Baur in directing attention to the fundamental agreement which from the first existed between

[1] ' Die Christuspartei in der korinthischen Gemeinde,' *Tübinger Zeitschrift für Theologie*, 1831, Heft IV. pp. 61 ff.

Jewish and Gentile Christians, and which the Tübingen school ignored, or are said to have ignored, without, by implication at least, extending our consideration to the relation borne by both parties, and especially by the former, to the old national creed and ceremonial. Baur and his critics are agreed in admitting that at any rate one party in the Church occupied a totally different ground from that of Judaism, and the greater the amount of harmony which can be made out between that party and the so-called Jewish Christians, the greater must have been the divergence of the latter from their ancestral position.

In a word, the greater the difference between Jewish and Gentile Christians, the greater must the similarity have been between Jewish Christians and Judaism, while, on the other hand, the greater the agreement between the former, so much the more real and important must the distinction between the latter have been. The following discussion will thus have to traverse a good deal of the well-trodden ground of the Tübingen school; and, as this school holds that two essentially different factors—Jewish and Gentile Christianity—became welded into the Catholic Church, the inquiry will have to be made here whether the Jewish Christians were originally almost indistinguishable from the Jews, as Baur's theory implies, and Dr Graetz, the learned historian of Judaism, maintains; and also whether the various sects and parties of Jewish Christians with which the post-apostolic age is full were—all or any of them—the representatives of early Christianity, or whether they were not rather the development of tendencies which were only latent in the early Church, and, in the prominence which they afterwards obtained, the product to a large extent of the religious and social upheavals of the time.

STATE OF JUDAISM. 5

But before going on to discuss these questions it will be necessary to give some account of the state of Judaism itself—its spirit and various sects and parties—at the time when Christianity arose.

Neither nationally nor doctrinally did Judaism any longer retain the homogeneity of its earlier years. Though the people may still have sought to preserve a united front against those without, previous dispersion and defeat had left no transient mark on their political unity. The wave of Western conquest on the crest of which Greece broke the narrow limits of the Aegean and extended its power and its culture to the then known world, had pierced the outer wall of partition that separated the Jews from surrounding races. The Jew abroad had already become a notable phenomenon in history; and, in addition to the old Hebrew race settled in Palestine, there arose Jewish settlers in Alexandria, Rome, and most of the great towns of the world, who, while maintaining their old religious worship and the purity of their race, became conformed to the language, and, in part, to the customs, of the people amongst whom they lived, and caught unconsciously their very mode of thought. The descendants of these Jewish settlers were, from their use of the Greek tongue, called 'Hellenists' to distinguish them from the 'Hebrews' of Palestine who still spoke a dialect of the ancient language. It was Hellenistic Jews that first carried the Gospel to the Gentile races, and to them Paul and Barnabas belonged. It was in consequence of an alleged neglect of their widows by the Hebrews that the first dissensions of the early Church arose, and it was the Hellenist Stephen—the most prominent of the seven deacons appointed to appease this discontent—who became the proto-martyr of the Christian

Church, and who is looked upon by Baur as the precursor of the Apostle Paul in his struggle with Jewish Christianity.

At the same time these Hellenists were not necessarily *Hellenizers* either in doctrine or custom. It is scarcely necessary to say that they are not to be identified with the 'Hellenists' of an earlier period, who, during the wars of independence against the Syrians, imitated the luxury and licentiousness of the Syrian Greeks and were rightly regarded by the other Jews as traitors to the covenant[1]. But the use of the Septuagint version of the Scriptures even by those of them who knew Hebrew, and of the Greek language for all ordinary purposes, not only made them susceptible to Western culture, but at the same time cut them off from the sympathies of their Palestinian brethren, from whose lips a modification of the old Hebrew speech was still to be heard, and who had no further literature than the Hebrew Scriptures and the interpretations by which they were beginning to be overlaid. And though many families—that of the Apostle Paul, for example—may have been as strict as any inhabitants of Jerusalem[2], yet, as a general rule, the Hellenistic Jews seem to have been less warmly attached to the rites associated with the Temple worship, as they certainly let them drop with less apparent difficulty after their adoption of Christianity[3].

Thus the suspicion with which Hebrew regarded Hellenistic Jew paved the way for that conflict between Jewish and Gentile Christians which well nigh rent the infant Church in twain. But the difference between them was, for the most part, one of sentiment and tendency rather

---

[1] Graetz, *Geschichte der Juden*, 2nd ed., III. 9.
[2] Phil. iii. 5; Acts xxvi. 5; Gal. i. 14; 2 Cor. xi. 22.
[3] Graetz, IV. 77.

than of creed and worship. Though the Alexandrians put the spiritual meaning of the Jewish ordinances above their formal observance, and though there may have been a tendency amongst some of them to treat the latter as indifferent, yet Philo, their greatest representative and one who used the allegorising method to its full extent, contends that we must be equally careful, both in the diligent search of what is hidden, and in the strict observance of what is revealed[1]. No two things, it is true, are more radically opposed than the philosophy of religion he cultivated and the corresponding science among the Pharisees of Palestine. The whole meaning of the two movements is different. The one is more Greek than Hebrew, breathes the spirit of philosophy rather than that of a positive historic religion, while the other is strongly opposed to the introduction of foreign elements, is unspeculative, exegetical, and founded on a worship of the letter. But the speculative tendency of the former is subtly interfused through a form of Scriptural interpretation, and thus clothed on with a semblance of the realities of the orthodox Jewish belief. Over their deeper differences there was thrown a superficial garb of agreement, and the philosophers of Alexandria, as well as the legalists of Jerusalem, fully acknowledged the authority of Moses and the prophets and obeyed all the behests of the law[2].

Not less important, however, than this want of national homogeneity among the Jews, was an inner difference amongst the inhabitants of Palestine itself which was more closely connected with their religious conceptions.

It would lead us too far afield to enter here into a thorough investigation of the character, relation to one

---

[1] *De migr. Abr., Opera*, ed. Mangey, I. 450.
[2] Cf. Neander, *Church History* (Engl. transl. 1847), I. 72.

another, and relation to Christianity, of the 'three philosophical sects,' as Josephus calls them[1], of the Pharisees, Sadducees, and Essenes. But traces of these different parties will so often meet us in the sequel, that it will be well to carry with us a picture in outline of their distinctive features. Much of the difficulty of portraying them arises from the fact that they were the gradual product of the political, religious, and, so to speak, literary experiences through which the Jews passed between the time of the Maccabees and the time of Christ, and when the voice of prophecy had long ceased to be heard among them. We must remember, too, that it is somewhat misleading to talk of them as 'sects' in the ordinary acceptation of the term. The strict distinction and definite doctrines implied by that name were, for a considerable time at any rate, unknown amongst them. The difference between them was only in the second place theological, and was primarily one of political and social aims. The Sadducees worshipped alongside of the Pharisees, and, if the Essenes had a separate and peculiar cult which excluded them from the Temple service, they differed from the Pharisees not so much in their ultimate object as by their despair of obtaining it in practical affairs, and their consequent attempt to realize their ideal of Judaism by a withdrawal from ordinary life. Besides, as Graetz points out[2], it is somewhat unfair to regard the Pharisees as a mere sect, since the mass of the people belonged to their party, and looked up to them as their religious leaders. For the Essenes lived apart from the main stream of Jewish life, while the Sadducees—whether from aristocratic contempt or from knowledge

---

[1] *Bell. Jud.* II. 8, § 2: Τρία γὰρ παρὰ Ἰουδαίοις εἴδη φιλοσοφεῖται, καὶ τοῦ μὲν αἱρετισταὶ Φαρισαῖοι κ.τ.λ. Cf. *Antiq.* XVIII. 1. § 2. Ἰουδαίοις φιλοσοφίαι τρεῖς ἦσαν ἐκ τοῦ πάνυ ἀρχαίου τῶν πατρίων.

[2] *Gesch. d. Juden*, III. 73; cf. Keim, *Jesus von Nazara*, I. 251.

of the world—seem to have relinquished the leading idea of Judaism, that of the divine guidance of their nation, and thus to have found themselves so thoroughly out of sympathy with the people that, though they were the political heads of the nation, and in possession of the higher priestly offices[1], popular feeling was so strong against them that they were compelled—so Josephus tells us—to conform to the doctrines of the Pharisees in their exercise of magisterial functions[2].

It had fallen to the Sadducees, who were at once the priests and nobles of the nation, to guide its fortunes through periods of military weakness and political dependence. "The Sadducees are the representatives of the new *state* which grew out of the rising under the Maccabees, the Pharisees are the representatives of the *community* whose foundation and whose end was the law[3]." As soldiers or statesmen the former had come to trust to individual exertion and to cast aside the doctrine of divine providence. Their views were thus conditioned throughout by opposition to the Pharisees of whose creed this belief was the key-note. The latter were the religious party in the nation, but opposed the political programme of the Sadducees. The Sadducees were the political party, but developed a theological position antagonistic to that of their opponents. They substituted individual free-will for the divine decree or $εἱμαρμένη$ (though the Pharisees had not regarded the two as inconsistent), and rejected

---

[1] The intimate connection of the priests with the Sadducees is plain from the way in which they are spoken of in the New Testament, e.g. Acts v. 17. That the Sadducees *were* the priestly party was asserted by Geiger in his monograph on 'Sadducäer und Pharisäer' first published in the *Jüdische Zeitschrift für Wissenschaft und Leben*, II. (1862). The same view was afterwards worked out with full and conclusive argument by Wellhausen, *Die Pharisäer und die Sadducäer* (1874). Compare Mr Robertson Smith's recent work, *The Old Testament in the Jewish Church* (1881), pp. 54, 62, 395.

[2] Jos. *Antiq.* XVIII. 1. § 4; cf. Keim, *Jesus*, I. 181 f.

[3] Wellhausen, *op. cit.*, p. 94.

the doctrine of the resurrection of the body[1]—Josephus says of the immortality of the soul[2]—by which the Pharisees vindicated their belief in the moral government of God. They seem to have also rejected the 'traditions of the elders[3]' or 'unwritten tradition[4]' which had gathered round the Scriptures and by which the Scribes interpreted and applied them. According to some early Christian accounts[5] they acknowledged the authority of no Scriptures except the books of the Torah, appealing to the letter of the Pentateuch as their standard, just as, at a subsequent period, the Karaites rejected the Talmud and fell back on the literal interpretation of Scripture, and as, from other motives, the Reformers cast aside the traditions of the Church and proclaimed the Bible to be 'the religion of Protestants.' Despite the dry, rationalistic tendency thus manifested, it is here perhaps—in their rejection of tradition—that we come upon the only point on which the early Christian community had any similarity to the Sadducees. And, after the destruction of Jerusalem, the Pharisees set themselves to defend their oral traditions against the Christians just as they had formerly had to defend them against the Sadducees.

Both with Pharisaism and with Essenism Christianity has more points of contact; and Christ himself has been asserted by one Jewish author[6] to have been an Essene, by another[7] to have been a Pharisee. Mr de Quincey too has made popular the notion that the early Christians were a party of Essenes; and, though the conclusion of the brilliant

---

[1] Matt. xx. 23; cf. Mark xii. 18; Acts xxiii. 8.
[2] *Bell. Jud.* II. 8. § 14.
[3] Παραδόσεις τῶν πρεσβυτέρων—N. T.
[4] Παράδοσις ἄγραφος—Philo and Josephus.
[5] Origen, Tertullian and Jerome; but cf. Wellhausen, p. 73 n.
[6] Graetz, in his *Geschichte der Juden*.
[7] Geiger; see p. 38 of the monograph cited above.

essayist was perhaps as much due to love of paradox and literary effect as to scientific conviction, the arguments of Graetz in support of a similar view call for closer examination. But if the predominantly religious view of things and the elevated morality of the Essenes, including their renunciation of the pleasures of the world, find their counterpart in Christianity, the practical and (without begging the question as to its universal application) missionary character of the latter has nothing to correspond with it in the retired life of the former; while the very idea of a Messiah, as well as the prophetic literature that enshrined it, seems to have remained unknown to, or unacknowledged by, the Essenes. And though their conception of a universal priesthood reminds us of the similar doctrine of the New Testament[1], the two priesthoods are far from identical in character: the excessively exact ritual of Essenism, its set prayers and sacrifices, lustrations and strict sabbatic observances, initiatory oath, minute regulations as to dress, and abhorrence of anointing oil, are all opposed to the freer spirit of the Gospel[2]; while its dualistic philosophy, with the mystic doctrines that followed in its train, and consequent rejection of marriage, indicate an entirely different standpoint from that of Christianity. The lavations of the Essenes have, it is true, been compared to the Christian baptism. But the latter is a ceremony performed once for all, and not a constantly recurring ordinance; besides—at any rate at a subsequent period and perhaps also before the time of Christ—baptism formed part of the initiatory rites by which outsiders were admitted into the Jewish covenant as Proselytes of Righteousness, and may have passed thence—but not from Essenism—into Christi-

[1] 1 Pet. ii. 5, 9; Rev. i. 6; cf. Ritschl, *Entstehung der alt-katholischen Kirche*, 2nd ed., p. 200.
[2] See especially Mark vii. 14—23.

anity. And even the voluntary poverty, and community of goods[1], on which Graetz seems chiefly to rely for establishing the Essenism of Christ, are not shown to be identical in the two. For, though Christ and those who accompanied Him on His journeys had doubtless a common purse[2], there is no reason to suppose that goods were held in common amongst those who did not travel with Him, but yet ranked themselves and were ranked by Him as His disciples. And even in the early apostolic Church the community of goods does not appear to have been compulsory upon all its members[3], but seems rather to have been the spontaneous reply of hearts newly touched by the feeling of a common brotherhood, than the result of any deliberate institution on the part of the leaders of the Church.

Even if we so far agree with Keim[4] in looking upon John the Baptist as forming the link between the Essenes and Christ, we must remember that John was radically distinguished from them by forsaking their contemplative life for the practical work of preaching, while his leading thought was the near fulfilment of that Messianic idea which they seem to have rejected. It would almost appear, indeed, that he had much more in common with the Zealots than with the Essenes. The Zealots arose out of the Pharisaic party, but what the latter held as a mere theoretic belief, their wild enthusiasm attempted to realize in present politics. "They were fanatics for God and the fatherland, not merely for God and the law[5]." And, though their

[1] The comparison on this point between the Therapeutae of Philo and the early Christian community as described in Acts ii. 14, 15, was already instituted by Eusebius, *H. E.*, II. 17.

[2] John xii. 6, xiii. 29.   [3] Acts v. 4.

[4] *Der geschichtliche Christus*, 3rd ed., p. 17; cf. his *Jesus*, I. 483, where John is said to have been 'nicht unmittelbar ein Essäer.'

[5] Wellhausen, p. 109.

political aims were transformed by him into a purely religious purpose, John's burning call to repentance and preparation for the kingdom of God, which roused the people of Judæa, was more nearly related to the 'Kingdom' they sought to realize than to the mystic piety of the Essenes.

Far greater, as it seems to me, was the similarity of Christ's standpoint to that of the Pharisees. For both occupied the common ground of the Jewish doctrine of the covenant God and the promised Messiah. In both was the idea of the Kingdom of God to which only righteousness admitted, though their righteousness rested on a strict observance of the minutiae of the law; that required by Him consisted in change of heart. On the subjects, too, of the resurrection of the body and of future retribution, Christ took the side of the Pharisees as against the Sadducees[1]. But the development of the law by the Scribes had consummated in a one-sided and narrowly intellectual conception of it which met with His strongest opposition[2]. He is distinguished from them above all by the spirituality of his idea of that Messianic Kingdom which it was His mission to found. And the uncompromising and even bitter antagonism with which He regarded them may perhaps be accounted for by the fact, that, having the idea before them, they or their leaders failed to recognise it in its true spiritual nature, obscuring both the Kingdom and its law —the one by their material conceptions, the other by their 'traditions,' the interpretations of the Halacha and Midrash. The old prophetic enthusiasm was no longer theirs; they were without the official rank that gave dignity to the Sadducees; and they strove to atone for the want of these by making use of their position as interpreters of the

---

[1] Keim, *Gesch. Christus*, pp. 20, 72.
[2] Matth. xi. 25 ff.: cf. Wellhausen, pp. 16, 21.

law. But in the minute regulations they devised, and the strict observances they enjoined, they so entirely missed its spirit as to encourage an inconsistency between outward conduct and spring of action,—the 'hypocrisy' which has become associated with the name of Pharisee.

Christianity thus grew up in an atmosphere charged mainly with Pharisaism, but interspersed with cross-currents of Sadducean indifferentism, and Essene ascetic mysticism, as well as of fanatic patriotism from the party of Judas Galilaeus, the founder of the so-called 'fourth sect' among the Jews.

In attempting to trace the relation which Jewish Christians bore to Judaism, it will be well to state clearly at the outset the sense in which the word 'Jewish Christians' is used. The natural signification of the term would seem to be Christians who were born Jews or who, before becoming Christians, had, as Proselytes of Righteousness, undergone the conditions and been admitted to the full privileges of Judaism. But in the ordinary theological use of the name, introduced mainly through the influence of the Tübingen school, it denotes a distinct party or sect of Christians, according to whom Christianity was conditioned by, or was indeed a mere supplement to, the national ideas and legal observances of Judaism. That the early Church was entirely Jewish Christian in the former meaning of the term is a simple matter of fact; that it was Jewish Christian in the latter signification is one of the chief theses of Baur and his followers.

Hence it seems to me unfairly to prejudice the questions under discussion if we start with the more special definition of 'Jewish Christian.' Besides, some name is required for those Christians—at first the whole number but afterwards a gradually decreasing proportion—who were either Jews by birth or who had been admitted such after circumcision, baptism and a sin-offering[1]. It will indeed be found advisable to restrict the meaning of the term in the sequel; but it is not necessary before starting to give a name to a definite view of Christianity which has not yet been met with and which may turn out to have arisen by slow degrees. If the meaning of the term 'Jewish Christian' becomes changed and specialized in the sequel from denoting Christians who had first been Jews to designate those who tried to continue Jews after becoming Christians, and to have all others enter the Church through the same gate of Judaism as they had done, the alteration will but correspond to the change of parties within the Church in relation to one another and in relation to their surroundings. At first the question was one of the relation of 'Jewish Christians' (i.e. Christians born Jews) to the Gentile converts on the one hand, and to the Judaism in which they had been brought up, and with which they had not expressly broken, on the other. Afterwards, when the rights of the Gentile converts had been vindicated, and for St Paul and many others there was neither Jew nor Gentile in Christ Jesus, the question became one of the relation of 'Jewish Christians' (i.e. Jewish Christians in the former sense who sought to retain their Judaism) to the rest of the Church (whether admitted by Jewish or Gentile gate) on the one hand, and, on the other, to the creed and constitution of that Judaism from which they were unwilling to separate themselves. These different phases of the question correspond broadly in time to the apostolic and post-apostolic ages respectively. And the division between the two periods

[1] The ceremonies of admission to Proselytism of Righteousness; cf. Graetz, IV. 110; Ferdinand Weber, *System der alt-synagogalen palästinischen Theologie* (1880), p. 75.

agrees pretty exactly with the date of the destruction of the Temple and dispersion of the Jews[1], events which formed a crisis in the history of Christianity as well as of Judaism. The following discussion thus falls naturally into two parts— the apostolic and the post-apostolic age, or that before and that after the destruction of the Temple—both because the relation between Jewish Christians and Judaism assumed different aspects during these two periods and because the authorities on which we have to rely in tracing that relation are different.

[1] The martyrdom of Paul and (?) Peter took place in 67, that of James the Just in 69; the Temple was destroyed in 70 A.D.

PART I.

THE APOSTOLIC AGE.

WE have here to depend almost entirely on the sources of information supplied from the Christian side. For the Jewish writers of the time—Philo and Josephus—pass over Christianity with a remarkable silence; while, for this whole period, the Talmud gives no account of the new phenomenon which had appeared on the scene of Jewish life[1]. Our knowledge of this part of the subject is thus derived, first, from the professedly historical records, the four Gospels and the Acts of the Apostles; secondly, from the Apostolic Epistles and the Revelation of St John, so far as they expressly deal with or unconsciously exhibit the relation of the early Christians to Judaism; and, thirdly, from any later accounts of the state of parties or customs of the time[2].

To the last class of authorities but little importance can be attached. They are valuable as unintentionally portraying the age in which they were written, rather than for any accurate information they give as to that they take in hand to describe. Destitute of the historic sense, their authors can be trusted only when confirmed by older writers, and then they are not needed.

[1] M. Joël, *Blicke in die Religionsgeschichte zu Anfang des zweiten christlichen Jahrhunderts* (1880), pp. ii., 29.
[2] Cf. Ritschl, *Alt-kath. Kirche*, 2nd ed., p. 108.

One of the best examples of this class of testimonies is the well-known account of James the 'Lord's brother' given by Hegesippus and preserved by Eusebius[1]. In this account characteristics predominantly Essene in their nature are, with great detail, ascribed to James the Just[2]; and, from this, large inferences have been made as to the practices of the early Church. It is well to remark, however, that even were the account to be entirely depended upon, it would only be the description of the idiosyncracies of an individual, not of the customs of a community. For the assertion of Graetz[3] that in these alleged peculiarities James was the model of the early Church is altogether without foundation in fact. But the story itself is unworthy of credit. For it contains traits altogether inconsistent with the customs of the Essenes (βαλανείῳ οὐκ ἐχρήσατο) as described by Josephus[4], as well as with what we otherwise know of James (ἔλαιον οὐκ ἠλείψατο) from the Epistle bearing his name[5], which has at least as good claims to be received as genuine as the account of Hegesippus has to be regarded as authentic. And from one sentence at any rate—τούτῳ μόνῳ ἐξῆν εἰς τὰ ἅγια εἰσιέναι—we can easily see how untrustworthy the whole account is. For the Temple was open not only to James, but to the apostles and to all the Jews. Nor can the story be defended by supposing that it was the inner sanctuary—the ἅγια ἁγίων—,

[1] *H. E.* II. 23.
[2] One of these characteristics—the abstinence from animal food—is also recorded of St Matthew, but by an even later authority, Clem. Alex.; cf. Ritschl, p. 224.
[3] *Gesch. d. Juden*, III. 250.
[4] 'Απολούονται τὸ σῶμα ψυχροῖς ὕδασι, Jos. *B. J.* II. 8, § 5. Schwegler (*Das nachapostolische Zeitalter*, I. 141), can only defend the above passage of the description by saying that James avoided all effeminacy.
[5] v. 14: ἀλείψαντες αὐτὸν ἐλαίῳ ἐν τῷ ὀνόματι τοῦ Κυρίου. What James recommended to others could hardly have been abhorrent to himself.

not merely the Temple, that was meant. For James was not of priestly race and thus could not have had either the exclusive entry or the entry at all into the holy of holies. The passage is only explicable on the supposition, either that when it was written James had already come to be regarded as having been high-priest[1], or that the Christians of the time and party from which the story emanated, were excluded from the national worship and thus came to fable it of James that he alone (of their sect) had been admitted to the Temple. In either case the historic back-ground of the picture shews it to have originated in the post-apostolic, not in the apostolic age.

Hegesippus, who flourished about the middle of the second century, is supposed by many critics to have belonged to the Ebionite party, and, whether this be the case or not, the description of James contained in his work is probably an Ebionite tradition, the author of which would no doubt be anxious to gain countenance for the customs of his sect by representing them as having been practised by James the Lord's brother who presided at the Council of Jerusalem mentioned in Acts xv., and who had already come to be looked upon at the time when Hegesippus wrote, or shortly afterwards, as having been, after the ascension of Christ, duly appointed by apostolic vote "Bishop of Jerusalem[2]." Just in the same way the pseudo-Clementine Homilies and Recognitions favour us with a description of Peter, different indeed in its details from the above, but springing from a similar motive and about as trustworthy.

[1] Epiphanius, *Adv. Haereses*, Haer. 78, §§ 13, 14.
[2] Heges. in Eus. *H. E.* II. 23: διαδέχαται τὴν ἐκκλησίαν μετὰ τῶν ἀποστόλων ὁ ἀδελφὸς τοῦ κυρίου ᾽Ιάκωβος· cf. Clem. Alex. in Eus. *H. E.*, II. 1. The above against Schwegler (*Nachap. Zeitalter*, I. 23), who says there is no ground for regarding the story of Hegesippus as fictitious.

For the materials of our investigation we are thus forced to fall back on the New Testament writings. These may be divided into two classes: (1) the professedly historical documents, the Gospels and the Acts of the Apostles; and (2) the other writings, including the Revelation of St John and the Epistles, the object of which is for the most part hortatory or doctrinal rather than narrative, though they contain historical information often only more valuable because recorded incidentally.

(1) The Acts might naturally be supposed to be the chief source of information for the history of the apostolic age; but unfortunately it is round that document that the chief difficulties of the investigation circle. As already stated at the outset, Baur's theory—by which this discussion is necessarily conditioned throughout—is an attempted reconstruction not only of the history of Christianity but of the Christian records, and its history of the period is founded on its criticism of these records. Now from his critical examination of the various New Testament writings, Baur thinks himself justified in concluding that the professedly historical works are not, in the proper sense of the term, histories at all, but writings in which words that were never spoken and actions that never happened are attributed to historical personages for the purpose of lending support to the views held by the author or the party to which he belonged. In the euphemistic language of German criticism they are *Tendenzschriften*,—all of them either taking a side in the conflict between Jewish and Gentile Christians or else aiming at a compromise between the contending parties. Thus the Gospel of Matthew is a 'Jewish Christian' document in which Christ is represented as coming to enforce and fulfil the law, that of Luke is a 'Gentile Christian' production according to which His mission was to

annul and abolish it, while the Gospel of Mark, relying upon both, acts as a mediator between them. The Fourth or Johannine Gospel, again, is the product of a time when the transition is being made to the Catholic Church[1], and in it the breach with Judaism is regarded as complete and even Paulinism is transcended[2].

But most of all have the Tübingen school subjected the Acts of the Apostles to a searching examination. And the works of Zeller and Schneckenburger are an evidence of the fact that they look upon its correct interpretation as the key to the whole history of primitive Christianity. It need hardly be said that they find it ruled by the old opposition of Paulinism and Petrinism, while its 'purpose' or 'tendency' is to bring the opposing parties together by means of a thorough-going manipulation, or rather distortion, of the whole history of the early Church, in which the words of Paul are put into the mouth of Peter, and actions which could have been performed only by the latter are attributed to the former—in which Paul is in many respects *Petrinized* and Peter systematically *Paulinized*.

If the Acts were written with this mediating tendency and unhistorical throughout, it seems to me inexplicable how, at the time when it appeared, it could have escaped criticism on that point from the Ebionites or extreme 'Jewish Christian' party who refused all compromise with the Gentile Christians. Yet so far were they from suspecting the authenticity or historical accuracy of this work, that Irenæus, writing about 180 A.D., could charge them with inconsistency for disparaging the authority of St Paul without rejecting the testimony of St Luke in the Acts

---

[1] Baur, *Kirchengeschichte der drei ersten Jahrhunderte*, 3rd ed., p. 147.
[2] Baur, *K. G.*, pp. 170 f.

according to which he was declared by God to be chosen to bear His name to the Gentiles[1].

Baur's theory of the untrustworthiness of the Acts is founded mainly on the alleged discrepancies between it and the historical details of Galatians i. and ii.; but though, I suppose, no competent critic will deny that the mutual relation of the two narratives raises points of very great difficulty, yet it would appear that if one theory of this relation is psychologically impossible it is the extreme view of the Acts adopted by the Tübingen school. Nor is this a question depending on the date at which that work may have been written. For the earlier its origin the greater number of persons would there be still alive who had taken part in, or at least had had accurate information from actors and eye-witnesses of, the real facts of the apostles' history, and the less likely would the author have been to fabricate a story whose falsehood could have been so easily detected and would infallibly have been exposed; while, on the other hand, the later its origin, the more public and widely known must the Epistle to the Galatians have become, and the more inconceivable is it that the author of the Acts should have deliberately and unnecessarily run counter (as, on Baur's reading of the document, he does on several occasions run counter both deliberately and unnecessarily) not only to apostolic authority, but to the evidence of one who had taken a leading part in the events he narrates.

At the same time, in the present state of critical opinion both as to the Acts and as to the Gospels, it is necessary

[1] *Adv. Haer.*, III. 15, § 1. This is not inconsistent with the information we owe to Eusebius (*H. E.* III. 27) and others that the only authoritative Scripture of the Ebionites was the Gospel of the Hebrews. The Ebionites did not look on the Acts as authoritative, but they do not seem to have suspected its historical character.

that the evidence drawn from them should not be indiscriminately mixed up with the testimony of writings whose genuineness and authenticity is universally acknowledged. It is true that, for a complete and ultimate discussion of the question, a critical examination of the authorities must first be carried through. But it is evident that such an inquiry, extending as it does over the whole field of New Testament Introduction, would be impossible here. And, if this essay has any value at all, it will be because it does not take postulates for granted which no opponent is likely to admit, but tries to reach its conclusions by starting from common ground and working along lines of argument the validity of which will not be denied.

(2) No critic, however bold, has attacked the genuineness of the leading Epistles of the New Testament Canon, and in relying upon them we are thus on safe ground. The four 'universally received' Epistles of St Paul — Galatians, First[1] and Second Corinthians, and Romans — would themselves enable us almost to reconstruct the history of Apostolic Christianity and the system of Christian doctrine, were the rest of the Canon lost. The Epistle to the Philippians, too, though rejected by Baur on account of its pronounced expressions on the divinity of Christ, is now generally admitted as the work of St Paul, while the tendency of recent criticism is to bring within the category of genuine writings other Epistles which bear his name. Thus Hilgenfeld, who is perhaps the most prominent living representative of Baur's critical school, accepts not only Philippians, but also First Thessalonians and the

---

[1] Graetz's rejection of 1 Cor. (*Gesch. d. Juden.* IV. 80 n.), founded as it is on a fanciful interpretation of a single phrase, has not found favour with critics. Besides, 1 Maccab. i. 15 shows that the practice referred to by Graetz was known long before the post-apostolic age.

Epistle to Philemon. The Epistle to the Hebrews, though not by Paul himself, was undoubtedly composed within a few years after his death. And according to Ritschl, who, in the second edition of his work on the 'Old Catholic Church,' frankly relinquished the Tübingen standpoint he had previously occupied, both the Epistle of James and the First Epistle of Peter can successfully vindicate their claim to apostolic authorship. These Epistles are of importance here as coming from the pens of the two disciples who stood, along with John, at the head of the early Church in Jerusalem. To the above writings we must add the Revelation of St John, which, written long before the Epistles and Gospel ascribed to him, is regarded by Baur as proving the Ebionite character and tendency of the primitive Christian community, and has thus great prominence given to it by him.

The works which will be chiefly drawn upon in the sequel are—for the above reason—those which all critics, whatever their theological leanings may be, are agreed in accepting.

The above discussion of authorities—tedious as I am afraid it may appear—will not have been misplaced if it has succeeded in obviating some preliminary difficulties and has made the way clear for exhibiting the points of relation between the Jewish Christians of the apostolic age and Judaism.

The development of this relation may be traced through three stages: 1°, There is the original element of difference which distinguished the first disciples from other Jews and in virtue of which they were Christians—an element not at first recognized by them in all its bearings and in its far-reaching implications, but which ultimately and necessarily broke through the outer web of external circumstance and traditional custom by which it was enveloped. 2°, There is this network of legal observances, adhered to by Jewish Christians equally with Jews, even when they saw how utterly it was bereft of significance by the new law of liberty they had come under, while it was regarded by the extreme party (by the 'Jewish Christians' in the sense of Baur) as essential to Christian communion. 3°, There is the process by which the new element introduced by Christianity and differentiating its adherents from unbelieving Jews separated itself from the ritual and customs of Judaism in the midst of which it had originated, and through conflict with these and schism within the Church itself, constructed an organization of its own which confirmed its separation from the parent stem.

These three stages do not of course follow one another in strict chronological sequence. The first and second are, indeed, naturally co-incident in time, while symptoms of the third stage, in which the two previous tendencies come into collision, begin to appear very early in the Church's history. They are rather elements which were never entirely separated in reality, though, by keeping them distinct in thought, we may gain a clearer view of the process by which the fulfilled Messianic idea perfected Judaism and annulled it, while those who had no eyes for this spiritual dialectic, but tried to remain both Jews and Christians, succeeded only, as Jerome says, in being neither Jews nor Christians.

1. It is hardly necessary to state that it was the recognition of Jesus as the Messiah that distinguished the believing disciples from their unbelieving fellow-countrymen. "Had no new development taken place," says Baur[1], the only difference between them "would have been that the former regarded the Messiah as having come already, the latter

[1] *K. G.*, p. 40.

looked on Him as still to come." And, could the belief in the Messiahship of Jesus be regarded as a mere abstract formula, this statement would be both accurate and complete. But one cannot help feeling it as a want in Baur's profound and suggestive treatises on early Christianity that the personal influence of the Founder over the thought and lives of his followers is not sufficiently acknowledged, or, rather, that the acknowledgment of it has not its full sweep allowed it in the development of the history. "How soon," exclaims Baur himself[1], "must all the true and weighty precepts of Christianity have been numbered with the faint echoes of words spoken by many a friend of humanity and philosophic sage of ancient times had not its doctrines been made words of eternal life in the mouth of its Founder." And again: "Had not the Messianic idea, the idea in which Jewish national hopes had their profoundest expression, fixed itself on the person of Jesus, and caused him to be regarded as the Messiah who had come for the redemption of His people, and in whom the promise to the fathers was fulfilled, the belief in Him could never have had a power of such far-reaching influence in history. It was in the Messianic idea that the spiritual contents of Christianity were clothed on with the concrete form in which it could enter on the path of historical development[2]." Two elements were thus necessary: the Jewish Messianic idea, and the personal character and influence of Christ. But all the evidence goes to show that He elevated and spiritualized it, rather than that it exercised a "cramping and narrowing" influence upon Him. We must remember too, that however much this idea may have been materialized and degraded during recent times when the independence of the state and revenge on the

---

[1] *K. G.*, p. 36. The translation is from the version edited by Mr Menzies.
[2] *Ibid.*, p. 47.

Romans were the highest thoughts and thus the Messianic idea of the leaders of the people, it had had a more spiritual meaning and a wider application in the golden days of Hebrew prophecy.

It is not contended that in the early Church there was a uniformly lofty Messianic idea. The gospel histories shew plainly enough how deeply the original apostles were imbued with the narrower conception of their time; but they also shew how persistently Jesus sought to widen and elevate it. But a decisive shock to the belief of many in the Messiahship of Jesus must have been given by the events which brought His earthly career to a close. A crucified Messiah was a stumbling-block to the Jews: a dead Messiah an impossibility. The disciples must either relinquish their belief in Jesus as the Messiah or they must also believe that in His own person He had conquered death. Even if they had seen nothing in Him before but the characteristics of a Hebrew prophet, those who remained faithful must acknowledge a unique virtue in the risen Christ. Thus it came about that the Messianic idea of the followers of Jesus had a real fulfilment, whereas that of the other Jews was a barren expectation, as well as a breadth of moral and spiritual content and a capacity for development which forced those who possessed it—or, rather, those who were possessed by it—far beyond Judaism.

This higher idea of Christ was not, of course, the *expressed* conviction of all his disciples, but it was *implied* in the Christian profession of the time, though there were no doubt various degrees in the measure of clearness with which it was recognized. No Jew could now be a Christian without believing in the resurrection of Jesus, and thus implicitly accepting all that that belief involved. It is true that the early disciples, even the apostles, may have expected a speedy return of the Lord from heaven and His assumption of temporal sway, but even the writings which go to prove that they did so are far beyond the standpoint of the Ebionitism which denied the supernatural and divine character of Christ.

The Apocalypse is one of the five New Testament writings accepted by Baur as genuine, and is regarded by him as occupying Ebionite ground. Yet that document lends no support to either of the two characteristic Ebionite views. For, on the one hand, it contains no word asserting the continued binding force of the law, while, on the other hand, it recognizes in the most distinct terms both the divine personality and the peculiar functions of Christ. He is there spoken of as 'the first and the last,' who is 'alive for evermore' (i. 17, 18), and who is worshipped by the four and twenty elders (v. 14). In many other passages He is directly associated with God; the great company of the redeemed cry 'salvation to our God which sitteth on the throne and unto the Lamb' (vii. 10); we read of those 'that keep the commandments of God and the faith of Jesus' (xiv. 12), and of those who 'shall be priests of God and of Christ' (xx. 6). He is further called the 'Lord of lords and King of kings' (xvii. 14; xix. 16). He is the $\dot{a}\rho\chi\dot{\eta}\ \tau\hat{\eta}\varsigma\ \kappa\tau\acute{\iota}\sigma\epsilon\omega\varsigma\ \tau o\hat{\upsilon}\ \theta\epsilon o\hat{\upsilon}$ (iii. 14), and even, in words which are sometimes regarded as having been introduced into Christian literature by the Fourth Gospel, as $\dot{o}\ \lambda\acute{o}\gamma o\varsigma\ \tau o\hat{\upsilon}\ \theta\epsilon o\hat{\upsilon}$ (xix. 13). That these are not mere titles affixed externally to Christ's person, as Baur somewhat perversely maintains[1], is shewn by the remarkable utterances as to His functions by which they are accompanied. He is the judge who sitteth on the white cloud 'having on his head a golden crown, and in his hand a sharp sickle' (xiv. 14), and who has 'the keys of death and of Hades' (i. 18). Still more remarkable is the significance attributed to the death of the

[1] K. G., pp. 316 f.

'Lamb...as though it had been slain' (v. 6). It is 'because of the blood of the Lamb' that the brethren 'overcame...the accuser' (xii. 11); and He is addressed as having 'loosed us from our sins by his blood' (i. 5; cf. v. 9, vii. 14). This is not the language of a leader of the Ebionites as Baur and Graetz maintain the Apostle John to have been[1].

It seems scarcely necessary to prove that similar views of Christ's person and work are held by St Paul. Yet Baur rejects the Epistle to the Philippians on account of its explicit teaching on the divinity of Christ. The same reason should have induced him to set all historical evidence at defiance and get rid of the four admitted Epistles as well. For in them Christ is regarded as 'the Son of God[2],' 'the Lord of glory[3].' He is also conceived as at once the Judge of the world—'we must all be made manifest before the judgment-seat of Christ[4]'—and the Redeemer who 'redeemed us from the curse of the law, having become a curse for us[5],' who 'hath been sacrificed' as 'our passover[6],' and in whom 'God was..., reconciling the world unto himself[7].'

The same conception of Christ as the paschal lamb which is found in St John and St Paul meets us also in the First Epistle of St Peter[8], who, along with John and James the Lord's brother, stood at the head of the early Church in Jerusalem; while, in their Epistles, both Peter and James seem to have passed beyond the stage in which observance of the Mosaic law was still looked upon as essential[9]: circum-

[1] Cf. Graetz, III. 250: 'Neben ihm [Jakobus dem Frommen] standen der ersten ebionitischen Gemeinde vor: Simon Kephas oder Petrus ben Jonas und Johannes b. Zebedaï.'
[2] Rom. i. 3, 4.
[3] 1 Cor. ii. 8.
[4] 2 Cor. v. 10; cf. Rom. xiv. 10.
[5] Gal. iii. 13.
[6] 1 Cor. v. 7.
[7] 2 Cor. v. 19.
[8] i. 18 f.: Εἰδότες ὅτι...ἐλυτρώθητε...τιμίῳ αἵματι ὡς ἀμνοῦ ἀμώμου καὶ ἀσπίλου.
[9] Cf. Ritschl, pp. 115, 119.

cision and Sabbath and feast-day are no longer regarded as requiring even mention.

Ideas such as the above are both far beyond the current Judaism of the day and far in advance of the conceptions of the so-called 'Jewish Christians' who sought to retain the Jewish standpoint along with a belief of some kind in Christ. The Ebionites held Christ to have been a mere man; not only Paul, but also the 'pillar-apostles[1],' ascribed to Him divine attributes. The former maintained that He had come to ratify and re-enact the law; the latter, in regarding Him as the paschal lamb slain for the sins of the world, held that He had fulfilled and abrogated it, introducing a new covenant in its stead[2].

"If," says Schwegler[3], "Christianity was looked upon simply as the continuation and last stage of the Old Testament Judaism, it follows that the person of Christ was placed only in the order and line of the Old Testament prophets." But since we have seen that the person of Christ was placed outside and above that order and line, we have on Schwegler's own premiss a right to conclude that, if Christianity is to be regarded as the last stage of Judaism, it was a last stage in which the whole previous history was summed up and transcended.

The documents from which the proof of these allegations has been drawn, belong, however, to the close of the apostolic age, and the doctrinal positions so clearly stated then were not necessarily present to the authors throughout the period, and were no doubt matured by the experiences they passed through. How far they underwent a process of development will, to some extent, appear when we come to consider the story of the conflict in which the new idea and

---

[1] Οἱ δοκοῦντες στῦλοι εἶναι, Gal. ii. 9.
[2] Cf. Ritschl, p. 122.   [3] *Nachap. Zeitalter*, I. 100.

old customs came into collision. But we may see in the early preaching of the resurrection and its historical consequences how from the first the original apostles were differentiated from the Jews.

(1) For, in the first place, the new creed had a missionary and aggressive character[1]. I am not speaking at present of the extent of these missionary operations of the primitive Church. But the very fact that the early apostles attempted in season and out of season to make converts marked them out as peculiar among Jewish sects. The Essenes lived by themselves; the Sadducees held aloof from the people; the Pharisees, secure in the adherence of the great body of the nation, appear not to have interfered much with the other sects[2]. And the apostles seem to have acted in defiance of all Jewish etiquette when 'every day, in the temple and at home, they ceased not to teach and to preach Jesus as the Christ[3].'

(2) The natural consequence followed: the early Christians were persecuted. Sadducees and Pharisees joined in an attempt to crush these new religionists who thus threatened 'to turn the world upside down[4].' Though this is both presupposed and asserted in the writings of St Paul, the direct evidence for the particular instances of persecution is, of course, taken from the Acts. But it is scarcely conceivable how even one who like Graetz denies its historical character, should assert that the relation between Jewish Christians and Jews was one of mutual toleration[5].

[1] Acts iv. 2, etc.
[2] Matth. xxiii. 15 seems to refer to proselytizing those outside Judaism, though Graetz, *Gesch. d. Juden*, IV. 109, says its meaning is still obscure. See, however, *ibid*. III. 211, 309.
[3] Acts v. 42.
[4] Acts xvii. 6.
[5] *Gesch. d. Juden*, IV. 88; but cf. III. 313.

It is hardly possible to believe that the coalition of Sadducees and Pharisees that procured the crucifixion of Jesus should have allowed His immediate followers openly to teach His Messiahship. It may, of course, be true that, after the conflict in the Church which followed the admission of Gentiles, the extreme Jewish Christian party may have been viewed with some favour by their unbelieving brethren; though, if so, the favour was of very short duration. But Gentiles were not admitted in any numbers to the Church till after the persecution that followed the death of Stephen, and disputed questions as to the terms of their admission do not seem to have arisen for some years subsequently. Nor is it at all likely that this persecution was aimed only at the Hellenists as Baur asserts[1]. For Paul, himself a Hellenist, was one of its leaders, and it was by Hellenists that the prosecution of Stephen, and, at a subsequent period, that of Paul, were initiated[2]. Nor, again, is Baur's other assertion that Stephen was the first opponent of Judaism[3]—if so, why did the 'Hebrews' leave it to the Hellenists to take action against him?—consistent with the remark he had just made, that he was condemned on the same grounds as Jesus.

(3) Brought together by their missionary operations and by the persecutions of hostile fellow-countrymen, the early Christians thus not only soon came to be looked upon as a distinct Jewish sect[4], but had from the first and were forced to develop an organization of their own, distinct from that of the Jewish community by which they were surrounded[5]. Formed on the analogy of the Jewish synagogue and pos-

---

[1] *K. G.*, p. 43.
[2] Acts vi. 9, ix. 29.
[3] *K. G.*, p. 42—3.
[4] Acts xxiv. 5.
[5] Cf. Rothe, *Anfänge der christlichen Kirche und ihrer Verfassung* (1837), pp. 146 ff.; and Cunningham's *Churches of Asia* (1880).

sessing its democratic constitution, this organization was yet sufficient both to increase the unity of the Christian party among themselves, and to signify to the world their difference from other Jews.

2. But while all this shows us how deeply the Messianic idea had taken root in the minds of the early disciples, how naturally and necessarily it led them outside the circle of Jewish observances, they still maintained their obedience to the Mosaic law and frequented the Temple worship. Their belief in the Messiahship of Jesus, which perfected their national consciousness and transcended it, did not seem to them to come into conflict with their national customs[1]. Perhaps it is no exaggeration to say that the early Christians were Jews first and Christians afterwards in more than the sequence of their own experience. They did not indeed value their Christianity less than their Jewish nationality; but they had not yet learned even in thought to separate them. It did not at first occur to them that the Messianic promise could be fulfilled to those who had never had the Messianic hope, or that the Gentiles could receive adoption into the new covenant, without passing into it, as they themselves had done, through the gateway of the old.

The early Christians had all been admitted by circumcision members of the old covenant, and they still retained the customs it involved: kept the Sabbath, observed the laws as to food[2], and frequented the worship of the Temple[3]—and that not merely from the opportunities of preaching it afforded[4]. In the appointment of the seven deacons they followed a practice usual in every Jewish community[5], while for the

---

[1] Cf. Baur, *Paulus, der Apostel Jesu Christi*, 2nd ed., I. 49.
[2] Acts x. 14.   [3] Acts ii. 46, iii. 1, etc.
[4] Acts xxii. 17, xxiv. 11—12.   [5] Graetz, III. 249.

peculiar institution of community of goods, which certainly prevailed for a considerable time and to a large extent among them[1], they had a precedent in the customs of the Essenes. Even their sacred rites of baptism and the Lord's Supper were founded upon Jewish ordinances[2]. But these rites now obtained a new meaning, and had an organic connection with the Christian principle, whereas the custom of circumcision, the laws of food, and the whole ceremonial regulations of the Mosaic law, had no natural or necessary relation to it, and thus lost their significance.

3. As long as the Church continued to consist entirely or almost entirely of Jews, the performance of these regulations would not be felt as an oppressive burden. But when the Gospel came to be preached to increasing numbers of Gentiles, the latter would be unable to see why in adopting the Christian principle they must needs submit themselves to Jewish customs, and a conflict was bound to ensue. The Church of Jerusalem had come to no decision beforehand as to how this emergency was to be met when it should arise. Their idea seems to have been that the Jews should first as a united nation be brought to recognize Jesus as the Messiah, and that the conversion of the Gentiles should only then be undertaken[3]. It is true that, according to the Acts, the older apostles not only preached the Gospel to the Samaritans (viii. 5 ff.), but Peter received Cornelius into the Church (x.), and Philip the Aethiopian Eunuch (viii. 27 ff.), and that simply by the rite of baptism and without subjecting them to

[1] Acts ii. 44 f., iv. 32 f.
[2] *Poverty*, it may be well to remark as against Graetz, III. 249, was not one of their characteristics (cf. Acts iv. 34), though it may have given a name to the Ebionites.
[3] Acts ii. 39; Rev. xiv. 4 (application of expression $\dot{a}\pi a\rho\chi\dot{\eta}\ \tau\hat{\omega}\ \theta\epsilon\hat{\omega}\ \kappa a\dot{\iota}\ \tau\hat{\omega}\ \dot{a}\rho\nu\iota\hat{\omega}$); James i. 18; cf. Ritschl, p. 141.

the conditions of the Mosaic law, though both the converts were mere Proselytes of the Gate (εὐσεβεῖς). But these actions are represented as having been undertaken by special revelation, and, even as it was, excited no little suspicion amongst, and even opposition from, the strict Jews, οἱ ἐκ περιτομῆς (xi. 23). There was, moreover, in their desire to win over to their faith their non-Christian Jewish brethren, a strong inducement for the early disciples, not to enter rashly upon a general proclamation of the Gospel to the Gentile races[1].

But what the apostles almost seem to have avoided came about without their connivance, and without their having the opportunity of prescribing the conditions under which it should take place. Amongst those driven from Jerusalem by the persecution which arose about Stephen were some 'men of Cyprus and Cyrene'—Hellenists therefore—who, on coming to Antioch, 'spake unto the Greeks[2] also, preaching the Lord Jesus' with such success that 'a great number that believed turned unto the Lord.' The importance of this step can hardly be over-estimated. What for Philip and Peter had been merely exceptional was thus made a general principle of conduct: the Gospel was not merely preached to the Gentiles—to Gentiles, too, who did not even conform to the conditions of Proselytism of the Gate, were not even εὐσεβεῖς—, but they were (as the history evidently implies) admitted into the Church without coming under the Mosaic law. The novelty of this proceeding excited some attention at Jerusalem—whether opposition as well does not at first appear—and the Church sent Barnabas, a Hellenist, to inquire into the state of affairs. His report was favourable, and no further action was taken in the matter; and it was not till

[1] Gieseler, K. G., § 28.
[2] Acts xi. 20—reading of course Ἕλληνας, not Ἑλληνιστάς (T. R.).

long afterwards that Paul had to vindicate against 'false brethren'[1] a similar liberty before the 'pillar-apostles' at Jerusalem.

Paul had been brought to Antioch by Barnabas just after the notable events of which that town had been the scene, had remained there a year, and, after a short visit to Jerusalem, had along with Barnabas undertaken his first missionary journey. It was on that journey, after repeated rebuffs from the Jews, that they openly announced their intention[2] of turning from them to what Paul regarded as his special mission[3]—the preaching to the Gentiles.

Between this decisive step on the part of Paul and the events related in Acts xv. and Galatians ii. a considerable interval elapsed[4] sufficient to allow the party in the Church which had gradually been forming time to take up definite ground against him.

In considering the events that followed as bearing on the relation held by the early Christians to Judaism, I shall restrict myself to the narrative of Paul himself in Galatians ii.

The Epistle to the Galatians, written between 54 and 57 A.D. and recording events which happened only two or three years before (according to Conybeare and Howson, in 50 A.D.), is the first authentic testimony we have of a party

---

[1] Gal. ii. 4.
[2] Acts xiii. 46; cf. xvii. 6.
[3] Gal. i. 16.
[4] The exact length of time is hard to determine, partly from the difficulty of saying whether the "fourteen years" of Gal. ii. 1 date from Paul's conversion or from his first coming to Jerusalem, partly from the Jewish method of reckoning, which makes "fourteen years" an ambiguous expression. I assume as proved the identity of the Jerusalem-visit of Gal. ii. with that of Acts xv. Both these subjects are fully discussed in Conybeare and Howson's *Life and Epistles of St Paul*, App. I. and App. III., Note (B); cf. Baur's *Paulus*, I. 120 ff.

in the Church which demanded that all Christians must conform to the ritual of Judaism—of 'Jewish Christians' in the technical sense of the Tübingen school, or, as they are otherwise called, 'Judaizers.' Baur says that 'Jewish Christianity' is here for the first time divided into a stricter and a broader party; but not only is it the case (as will soon be shewn) that only one of the parties here deserves the name of 'Jewish Christian' in his sense of the term, but 'Jewish Christianity' itself (in this sense) now for the first time makes a public appearance. The tendencies which it represents must no doubt have been all the while present, though latent, in the Church at Jerusalem; but that they were not the prevailing sentiments is shewn not only by their having been expressed by no one individual whose name is known to history, but also by the fact that (whether we accept the testimony of the Acts or not) the admission of Gentiles to the Church must have been carried on by Paul and his companions for a considerable time before their proceedings were challenged.

At the conference at Jerusalem—fraught with such important consequences for the future that it is usually spoken of as the first Christian Council—there were, besides the heads of the Church there (James, Peter and John), two opposing parties occupying a perfectly intelligible but mutually antagonistic position. There was the 'Jewish Christian' or 'Judaizing' party who contended that the Gentiles must keep the whole Mosaic law and, as an example and pledge of this, demanded the circumcision of Titus, a young Greek convert whom Paul had brought with him. This initiatory rite always entailed the performance of the remaining conditions of the law, and, without it,—the Jewish doctors taught[1]—the fulfilment of these is unavailing, for the

[1] Ferd. Weber, *op. cit.*, p. 66.

law which brings life to Israel is death to the heathen. In demanding the circumcision of Titus, therefore, this party demanded the *Judaizing* of the Gentile Christian churches which Paul was so successfully building up. This demand was not only refused in the most uncompromising manner by the apostle of the Gentiles, but those who made it were stigmatized by him as 'false brethren privily brought in who came in privily to spy out our liberty.' They had evidently gone up to Antioch to inspect Paul's doings there and had thus made him determine on his journey to Jerusalem[1] to explain κατ' ἰδίαν to the leaders of the Church there (τοῖς δοκοῦσι) the gospel he preached to the Gentiles. The view on which he acted was that the Christian principle had made circumcision and all such ordinances matters of indifference. But he made no demand for the Church at Jerusalem to throw off Jewish customs. On the contrary, in an Epistle written at no great distance of time from this, he says that to the Jews he himself became a Jew that he might gain the Jews[2]—a remark which may or may not refer to an occasion on which, according to Acts xxi. 26, he actually did so, but which certainly stamps with his approval the conduct of the congregation at Jerusalem in conforming to Jewish customs as long as they had the hope of gaining over their brethren.

From some expressions he uses, Paul seems to have been doubtful as to the course the older apostles would take on the question at issue. But, on the only point before them, they decided thoroughly in his favour, being convinced that the work done by him among the Gentiles had as certain an evidence of divine approval as the work done by them among the Jews, that an εὐαγγέλιον τῆς ἀκροβυστίας had been com-

---

[1] This is of course not inconsistent with his own view that he went up κατὰ ἀποκάλυψιν, Gal. ii. 2.
[2] 1 Cor. ix. 20.

mitted to him just as the εὐαγγέλιον τῆς περιτομῆς had been entrusted to Peter, since the same spirit worked in both[1]. And it is almost inconceivable how, in the face of this, Baur should say[2] that Paul's doctrine of freedom from the law separated him from the 'pillar-apostles' as well as from the Jews, or should have committed himself to the statement that if the older apostles agreed with the principles of Paul's εὐαγγέλιον τῆς ἀκροβυστίας it was their duty to turn their attention henceforth to the conversion of the Gentiles[3] (leaving, I suppose, the Jews to their fate), as if the division of apostolic fields of labour were inconsistent with unity of apostolic aim and spirit.

The only condition Paul records as having been exacted by the older apostles, and one which was cordially accepted by him, was that the Gentile churches he founded should not relinquish that custom inherited from Judaism, and which has never ceased to be distinctive of the Christian Church—the care of the poor—, and should give proof of their unity and sympathy with the Palestinian Jews by helping to relieve the distress which famine had caused among the poorer brethren of Judaea.

According, however, to the account given in Acts xv., a formal decree was issued on the occasion ratifying the Christian liberty of the Gentile churches but also requiring their abstinence from certain Gentile customs which were particularly obnoxious to Jews, and which had probably been made the subject of special complaint by the Judaizers, the conditions enjoined being, perhaps, though the point is not quite clear, the same as those exacted from Proselytes of the Gate.

It is not my intention to enter into the controversies which surround this decree, for it is of importance in tracing

[1] Gal. ii. 7, 8. [2] *Paulus*, I. 223.
[3] *Paulus*, I. 144.

the relation of the Jewish to the Gentile Christians rather than that of the Jewish Christians to Judaism[1]. But although St Paul makes no express mention of it in his Epistles, his subsequent conduct seems to imply that an edict of the kind had been issued for the temporary guidance of the Gentile Christians in relation to their Jewish brethren[2].

Undiscouraged by defeat, the 'Judaizers' did not relinquish their contention on account of what had happened at Jerusalem. Shortly after the events already recorded Peter seems to have followed Paul to Antioch probably with the intention of giving, by his personal presence among them, the sanction of the older apostles to the Gentile Christian community at that centre. At any rate we find him there taking part in the full social as well as religious fellowship which, no doubt through Paul's influence, had been established between the Jewish and Gentile members of the Church. Peter thus fell in with their new customs, till 'certain came from James' and, in the interests of so-called 'Jewish Christianity,' succeeded in causing an unseemly quarrel in the Church.

It is doubtful whether these Jews were sent to Antioch by James; but even if they were, there seems no reason for supposing that they were commissioned by him to play the part they did[3]. We do not know what arguments they made use of when they appeared at Antioch; but we may well believe that they did not now insist explicitly, as they had but recently insisted, on the *Judaizing* of the Gentile

---

[1] For the same reason no attempt is made here to discuss the questions raised as to the relation of Acts xv. to Gal. ii. To do so would lead into controversies almost interminable, and for all the purposes of this essay the narrative of Paul himself in the Galatians is sufficiently full.

[2] Cf. Ritschl, pp. 137 f.

[3] So Baur himself in his early essay on the 'Christuspartei,' *Tüb. Zeits.*, 1831, iv. p. 114.

Christians. They would, probably, rather take up the plea of following out literally the decision of the Council of Jerusalem, and assert that it was specially incumbent on Peter as the representative of the εὐαγγέλιον τῆς περιτομῆς to maintain the Jewish customs and refuse to sit at table with the Gentiles, and that all who were of Jewish birth should do the same. It is obvious, however, that, although Peter may have advanced beyond the regulations of the decree, he had acted fully in accordance with the spirit of a resolution which relegated Jewish customs to the class of things non-essential. But, with a weakness which cannot be said to be inconsistent with what we otherwise know of him, he yielded to the pressure and followed the intolerant example of the Judaizers, who led astray the other Christian Jews and even the Hellenist Barnabas 'by their dissimulation (ὑπόκρισις)[1].' It was then that Paul 'withstood Peter to the face' (ii. 11): the apostle of the ἀκροβυστία came into conflict with the apostle of the περιτομή. The tragic interest of this episode in which, not thirty years after its first promulgation, the two leaders of the religion of peace and brotherly love are seen face to face in open[2] feud, has naturally attached to it a

[1] Gal. ii. 13. It is not necessary here to discuss the quarrel mentioned in Acts xv. 37, 38 between Paul and Barnabas, because the latter 'determined to take with them John whose surname was Mark,' whereas 'Paul thought not good to take him with them who departed from them from Pamphylia' (cf. Acts xiii. 13). Dr John Lightfoot supposes that the defection of Mark was due to the fact that, as a follower of Peter, he "liked not what these ministers of the uncircumcision did among the Gentiles" (*Exercitations upon the First Ep. to the Cor.*, i. 12—*Works*, XII. 457, ed. of 1822—5). This is an interesting suggestion not only as obviating Baur's objection to the cause of the quarrel given in Acts xv. 37, 38, but as showing that the importance of the distinction between the two parties in the Church could be recognized by one who wrote more than a century and a half before the way had been paved for the Tübingen theory by modern critical methods and the Hegelian philosophy.

[2] Ἔμπροσθεν πάντων, Gal. ii. 14.

greater significance than its theological importance merits. Even in the early Corinthian Church we read of a Paul-party and a Peter-party, while amongst some modern critics Paulinism and Petrinism almost become the names of different religions. Perhaps this exaggeration is inevitable, but it is certainly an exaggeration. Not that the question at issue was a small one: far from it. But at the same time its importance does not seem to have been nearly so great as that of the point settled at Jerusalem. Nor did Peter's weakness now mean the retractation of the decision he had given them. His action on this occasion is regarded by Paul himself as one simply of cowardly inconsistency between his conduct and the principle he had adopted; while a full identity of doctrinal position between the two apostles is assumed in the argumentative verses that follow his account of the dispute (ii. 16—21).

Besides, the most noticeable fact in the story is not that Peter withdrew from the table at which the Gentiles sat, but that he went to it at all[1]—a point which Baur passes over. For, in so doing, he showed that in his eyes the meaning of the decision given at Jerusalem was not simply that Jewish and Gentile Christians "agree each to go their own way independent of the other[2]," but that it contained the acknowledgment that their common Christianity was a more fundamental principle and closer bond of union than the exclusive customs which bound Jew to Jew, and that, when the two came into collision, the latter should give way to the former. It was for unfaithfulness to this testimony—a testimony, however, which, once given, could not be revoked by

---

[1] The agreement of his conduct in so doing with what he is recorded to have said Acts xv. 7—9 deserves notice.
[2] Baur, *K. G.*, p. 51.

mere inconsistency—that Peter incurred the stern censure of his brother apostle.

The terms in which the censure was conveyed have been differently understood. "If thou," said Paul, "being a Jew, livest as a Gentile, and not as a Jew (ἐθνικῶς ζῇς καὶ οὐκ Ἰουδαϊκῶς), why forcest thou the Gentiles to Judaize" (Ἰουδαΐζειν)[1]? But though our imperfect information makes it difficult or impossible to tell to what the reference may be, the plain reading of the words seems to imply that Peter as well as Paul had departed from the strict observances of Jewish ritual in more than this matter of social intercourse with the Gentiles from which he was now drawing back. We further learn from the passage that Paul clearly saw that the consequence and tendency of Peter's behaviour, if unchecked, would have been not the mere social separation of Jewish from Gentile Christians, but the attempt to exact from the latter the observance of the whole Jewish law.

The immediate upshot of this controversy is unknown, and the subsequent career of the Jewish Christian party during the apostolic age has to be made out from the slightest hints. It is evident, however, from what has been already said, that the older apostles did not agree with the demands of the extreme party—representatives of which were to be met with in the Jewish Christian communities of Asia Minor, Greece and Rome as well as in Palestine. In refusing to have communion with or to acknowledge as Christian brethren the Gentile Christians who would not keep the law, this party was driven into bitter antagonism to St Paul who had to defend his very apostleship against attack[2]. That in this conflict the Judaizers were altogether separated from the sympathies of the older apostles is suggested by the previous narrative and is proved by the

[1] Gal. ii. 14.   [2] 1 Cor. ix. 1 ff.

manner of St Paul's defence. For, while those who led the Corinthians astray are denounced by him as false apostles[1] and false brethren, the original apostles are merely spoken of as if they had been over-rated—$\dot{v}\pi\epsilon\rho\lambda\dot{\iota}a\nu$ $\dot{a}\pi\dot{o}\sigma\tau o\lambda o\iota$ he calls them[2]—by being placed above himself who also held his commission direct from the Lord.

The new faith professed by the apostles had to vindicate its position as the historical representative of the religion of Israel. It must find in itself an explanation of, if it did not continue, the prophetic, the legal, and the priestly orders. And these different parts of the Old Testament doctrine are brought into prominence by different writers in the New. Thus it has been said that for Peter the fulfilment of prophecy is the fundamental thing in Judaism; for James, and, in a different way, for Paul, the fulfilment of the law; while the author of the Epistle to the Hebrews looks from the point of view of the priesthood and the atonement it effected[3].

In the earlier and simpler stages of the Old Testament religion there does not seem to have been any distinction between these different systems. The prophet Moses was at the same time both lawgiver and priest, while the specialization of functions and the growth of a legal and of a priestly caste were the work of a later time and corre-

---

[1] 2 Cor. xi. 13.

[2] 'So sind wohl die $\dot{v}\pi\epsilon\rho\lambda\dot{\iota}a\nu$ $\dot{a}\pi\dot{o}\sigma\tau o\lambda o\iota$ die Apostel selbst deren Schüler und Abgeordnete zu seyn, die $\psi\epsilon v\delta a\pi\dot{o}\sigma\tau o\lambda o\iota$ vorgaben.'—Baur in *Tüb. Zeits.*, 1831, IV. p. 103. The reference of the $\dot{v}\pi\epsilon\rho\lambda\dot{\iota}a\nu$ $\dot{a}\pi\dot{o}\sigma\tau o\lambda o\iota$ to the older apostles is disputed by Beyschlag (*Studien und Kritiken*, 1865, II. 227) and others, while Baur afterwards held, and in this he is followed by the Tübingen school generally, that not only it but also the $\psi\epsilon v\delta a\pi\dot{o}\sigma\tau o\lambda o\iota$ is levelled at them.

[3] Weiss, *Lehrbuch der biblischen Theologie d. N. T.* (1868), § 138, p. 511.

sponded to the needs of a more complex society. A similar sequence of ideas may perhaps be traced in the young Christian community. At first Christ is received both as a 'prophet like unto Moses,' and as the Messiah-king to whom the later prophetic literature pointed. But it was only afterwards, under the sharp edge of controversy, that the attitude of the new religion to the developed Mosaic law and levitical ritual was brought into prominence. Hence the conflict of St Paul with the legalism of the Judaizing Christians; hence too the endeavour of St James to enforce the moral content of the Christian 'law of liberty' at once against the formalism of the Jewish law, and the antinomian followers of St Paul, to whom liberty meant licence, and who, knowing no law but the Jewish, thought that its abrogation meant the dissolution of all moral ties.

Still later, the relation of Christianity to the old levitical system is dealt with in a document which, steeped in the ideas of sacrifice and priesthood, has had more influence on Christian theology than any other New Testament writing except the Epistle to the Romans. It is true, as has been already pointed out, that conceptions borrowed from the levitical order are applied to Christ in the works of the apostles[1]. But their general point of view is not the priestly, but the prophetic or the legal; whereas, in the Hebrews, we meet with an author who looks upon Judaism as, in its essence, a priestly system in which man is reconciled to God through sacrifice, and who consciously sets before himself the question, What is the significance of this system in the light of the Christian principle? It is not necessary to assert, as Geiger so confidently does, that the author of the Epistle had been a Sadducee. Geiger says that Pharisaism, which made its influence first felt on

[1] Rev. i. 5, v. 9; 1 Cor. v. 7; 1 Pet. i. 18, 19.

the Christian Church, contributed to it the Messianic idea and the belief in the resurrection, while Sadducees, in coming over to the young community subsequently, brought with them the conception of the Messiah as the High-Priest who by His own death made atonement for sins. This is, according to Geiger[1], the fundamental idea both of the Hebrews and of the so-called 'Testaments of the Twelve Patriarchs' which will come before us again in the sequel. But, in the first place, the belief in the resurrection and the prominent angelology exhibited by the Hebrews are difficult to reconcile with the hypothesis of its being of Sadducean authorship[2]. And further, the argument of the Epistle — the levitical high-priesthood superseded by an eternal High-Priest, the daily sacrifice for atonement rendered unnecessary by a world-sacrifice once offered by Jesus—does not require a Sadducee to have written it. For a sense of the importance of, and reverence for, the Temple services were not confined to the Sadducees, who were only the leaders and official members of a system which had sunk deep into the national consciousness. And it is not unnatural to suppose that a pupil of St Paul, inspired with his master's idea that the law which led to Christ was of no further value, should apply a similar train of thought to the great sacrificial system of the Temple.

Following out some such conception as this, the author looks on the Old Testament ritual as consummated in the death of Christ; and it is just here that the interest of his work for our subject lies. Riehm sees in the writer's argument evidence of the fact that "when he received the knowledge of Christ's work of salvation, he must have been already convinced of the inefficiency of the Old Testament sacrifice,

[1] *Jüdische Zeitschrift*, VII. (1869), pp. 119 ff.; XI. (1875), p. 16.
[2] Cf. *Jüd. Zeits.* VIII. 164 f.

and accustomed to a higher consideration of the ceremonies of Judaism, so as to join on his Christian doctrine to his pre-Christian views as the last stage of their development[1]." The Epistle thus shews how it is of the very essence of the old ritual that it should be done away with in the perfect sacrifice of Christ's life and death, and calls upon the Christian community it addresses to separate itself from Judaism and follow Christ 'without the camp[2].' The exact significance of this striking utterance depends both on the circumstances of those addressed—, whether or not they were inhabitants of Jerusalem—, and on the time at which it was written—whether before or after the destruction of the Temple. The references the author makes to its services are thought by some to imply that they were still going on when he wrote, while others hold that the termination of the Jewish sacrificial system is presupposed in his point of view. It would be inconsistent with the plan of this essay to attempt to decide between these two opinions, or to discuss the literary questions of the date and destination of the Epistle. But, whether occasioned by the threatened dissolution of the national worship or by its actual fall, the natural interpretation of the passage seems to be a clear call to the Christians of Jewish birth who still continued to reverence the ritual of the Temple, as well as to observe the worship of the Church, to come out and formally separate themselves from a system which had been consummated when Jesus was led 'without the gate' to be crucified.

But while this was the attitude towards Judaism to which the catholic thought of the church tended, we have

[1] *Lehrbegriff des Hebräerbriefes*, new ed., 1867, p. 627.
[2] xiii. 13 : Τοίνυν ἐξερχώμεθα πρὸς αὐτὸν ἔξω τῆς παρεμβολῆς.

already seen that unanimity of sentiment and conduct did not exist among its members. The preceding discussion has brought to light, in the apostolic age, three parties—as, for want of a better name, they may be called—of Christians who were born Jews. There were, first, the extreme Jewish Christians who not only observed the law themselves, but required that all Christians should do so; secondly, the original apostles and those who agreed with their position; and, thirdly, Paul himself with his adherents throughout the various churches he founded. He contended not merely for the freedom of the Gentile Christians from the Jewish law but also for the liberty of the Jewish born Christians of the same community to hold fellowship with their Gentile Christian brethren. His enemies at Jerusalem asserted that he taught men everywhere against the Jews, their law, and their temple[1]; and though, as they put it, this part of the accusation is no doubt as false as its sequel that he polluted the Temple by bringing a Greek into it, we can easily see that in one sense it was perfectly true. Paul's doctrine was opposed to the λαός inasmuch as he regarded the Gentiles as co-heirs of the Christian inheritance, and himself expressly, in his teaching, turned from the Jews to them. It was opposed to the νόμος, for he encouraged the Gentile converts to disregard it and even did so himself; and it was opposed to the ἅγιος τόπος, for the independent worship of his religion rendered its ritual unmeaning and its sacrifice an anachronism. And although he could himself conform to Jewish customs when expediency required it[2], he had evidently thrown off altogether the authority the law once had over his conscience, regarding it as no more than the pedagogue who had led him to the school of Christ and

---

[1] Acts xxi. 28; cf. xxiv. 6.
[2] Acts xvi. 3, xxi. 26; cf. 1 Cor. ix. 20.

whose services could be dispensed with once he had entered its door[1]. The stages by which the remaining Jewish customs were abolished in the churches founded by him cannot be traced. The first step having been taken in violating the laws as to food, the other observances were probably discontinued by insensible degrees. It is certain at any rate that they very soon disappeared. Though the Paulinists had to contend with Judaism both within the Church and outside of it, it soon ceased to exist as a motive force in their own experience, and the name 'Jewish Christian' can no longer be rightly applied to them.

Of the original apostles and their followers at Jerusalem it is harder to speak with certainty. Probably they continued to the end—as their Master had done before them[2] —to observe the customs of the Jewish law. Occasion has already been taken to dispute the accuracy of a description of James the Just by a writer of the second century. But the legend enshrined by Hegesippus had no doubt its foundation in fact, and the life he professes to depict may well have been one of strict legal observance and even of levitical purity. Yet, as has been pointed out, both James and Peter seem in thought to have got beyond the observances which they still continued to practise, and, in their Epistles, the particularity of the Jewish law has been done away with by, and resolved into the universal obligatoriness of, the higher 'law of liberty[3].' Their position does not seem to have differed theoretically from that of St Paul, for they admitted, as has been shewn, that the law was not absolutely binding. But, at the same time, their practice was

[1] Gal. iii. 24.
[2] See Justin Martyr's explanation of Christ's observance of the law. *Dial. cum Tryphone*, c. 67.
[3] James i. 25, ii. 12.

perhaps nearer that of the Judaizers than his. They thus occupied a middle position between the two extreme parties. But there is no ground for supposing that they meant this attitude to be permanently held to. It was temporizing and therefore temporary. It was adopted not to solve the question of the relation of Christianity to Judaism, but to stave off a pressing difficulty, so that the question might have scope given it to work out its own solution in the natural course of events. And it is therefore not to be wondered at if the party who persisted in occupying this position after the close of the apostolic age made no striking and independent place for themselves in history.

The extreme Jewish Christian party, on the other hand, refused all compromise with the Gentiles admitted into the Church—both kept the law themselves and insisted that everyone else should do so. But, though it is certainly "established beyond doubt" as Pfleiderer says[1] "that the dogmatic standpoint of Paul's doctrine and that of the Jewish Christians were antagonistic in principle," the preceding discussion has shewn that it cannot be established in any way whatever that the position of these Jewish Christians in this matter was identical with that of the original apostles, or that the opinions of the latter were antagonistic in principle to those of St Paul. We are thus not surprised to find that, by the extreme views they adopted and their bitter opposition to St Paul, these Jewish Christians soon sank into the position of a sect, and, at the same time, seem to have fallen back into, if they ever got beyond, the doctrines of that Judaism whose customs they could not be induced to relinquish. And, although the 'Judaizers' we have met with as yet were 'of the sect of the Pharisees[2],' it would seem that,

---

[1] *Paulinism*, Eng. tr., II. 23.
[2] Acts xv. 5.

RESULTANT STATE OF PARTIES. 51

even before the close of the apostolic age, some of them had begun to fence about their position with the ascetic practices and perhaps also with the dualistic philosophy of the Essenes[1], or that members of that sect converted to Christianity had brought their old customs and views with them into the Church[2]. However this may be, these tendencies appear clearly enough in the post-apostolic age, and it is not till then that 'Jewish Christianity' is to be seen in full development.

[1] Rom. xiv. 21; Col. ii. 16 ff.; cf. Baur, *Paulus*, I. 383 f., and Ritschl, p. 232 f.

[2] It is noticeable that these tendencies appeared first at Rome and Colosse, not at Jerusalem where the 'Jewish Christians' seem to have remained Pharisaic till the destruction of the Temple brought them into contact with the Essenes.

PART II.

THE POST-APOSTOLIC AGE.

It is a mistake, as Baur remarks[1], to separate the apostolic from the post-apostolic age as if there were any want of historical continuity between the two, and the development of the latter did not find its sufficient explanation in the tendencies already at work in the former conjoined with the external circumstances conditioning their growth. But, while this is eminently true of the Christian Church, the circumstances which marked off the two periods from one another were such as to cause something very like a break, and to necessitate a new beginning, in the history of Judaism. The development of the Church, external as well as internal, went on almost as before after the removal of the apostles from its head. The real separation of the two periods—apostolic and post-apostolic—is not the death of Peter and Paul and James the Lord's brother somewhat before 70 A.D., or of John about thirty years afterwards, but is that event which shook Judaism to its foundations and, in a different way, profoundly affected the Christian Church—the destruction of the Temple.

To the Jews this was an event of terrific significance. Both politically and religiously, it seemed to mean their

[1] *K. G.*, p. 130.

extinction. With the exception of the brief outburst under Bar Cochba sixty years later, it did put an end to their existence as a state; for any other people, perhaps, it would also have been the death of their distinctive religion. But the want of political organization, and, very soon, of home and fatherland, seems almost to have intensified the national life of the Jews; while the demolition of the only place in which the most sacred rites of their worship could be solemnized but drove them back on the moral truths which underlay their religious ceremonies, and made them seek a new pathway for the development of their creed. With a tenacity of life which only Jews could exhibit, they turned the current of their national existence into a new channel, and, with a wonderful instinct, they chose for it the course which subsequent history has shewn to be a better guard of national unity and racial purity than the strongest geographical frontier or the most compact political constitution. The study and development of the law now gained full supremacy over the other elements of Judaism. Priest as well as Prophet gave way to the Wise Man and the Scribe: the theocracy became merged in a nomocracy[1]. And hence, if the *sacrificial* temple on Mount Moriah was levelled with the ground, its place was supplied by a *doctrinal* temple, built, like the former, without sound of hammer or of axe, but which no hostile force could overthrow; and if victims slain for the sins of the people no longer smoked on their altar, yet, at all times and from all places, the supplications of the chosen race could still ascend to Him who would "call their prayers sacrifice[2]."

It is to Rabbi Jochanan, a pupil of Hillel, that the credit

[1] Weber, *op. cit.*, pp. 59 f., 122.
[2] Justin, *Dial.* c. 117. Prayer was regarded by the Jews as taking the place of sacrifice.—Graetz, IV. 72.

is due of having saved Judaism by yielding its political existence when opposition was hopeless, and bargaining for the continuance of its intellectual life. He obtained from Vespasian permission to set up a school at Jabne or Jamnia, a town on the coast of the Mediterranean between Joppa and the former Philistine settlement of Ashdod. There Jochanan devoted himself to the "Talmudism" of which Hillel was the founder—to the illustration and application of the precepts of the law—and there his successors continued their labours till they had to flee from the persecution which followed Bar Cochba's unsuccessful revolt.

Doctrine thus became "the soul of Judaism[1]," the centre and the spring of all that was noblest in its subsequent history. It is hardly too much to say that it henceforth began to be less and less a religion, more and more a philosophy. The old aristocracy was abolished by the fall of the state; the priesthood had lost its function and its place with the destruction of the Temple. But the influence of the scribes or doctors of the law, resting on no such external supports, was only increased by the downfall of the rival levitical power. While this, however, was the only way in which Judaism could develop as a living system, the Jews themselves were variously affected by the victory of Vespasian. The mass of the people, carried away into captivity and sold as slaves, maintained their religious peculiarity as the exiled Jew had long ago learned to do. But when the few who were left behind saw the pledge of the divine presence destroyed before their eyes, it was only a section that followed the lead of R. Jochanan, while others, dispersed in Syria and in Judæa, either betook themselves to an ascetic life, or found a substitute for their abolished sacrificial ritual in the Christian faith. The poll-tax ($\phi \acute{o} \rho o s\ \tau \hat{\omega} \nu\ \sigma \omega \mu \acute{a} \tau \omega \nu$)

[1] Graetz, v. 155.

levied against the Jews by Vespasian and afterwards cruelly exacted by Domitian, may also have induced others to hide their Judaism in the new community; while the Essenes, as will subsequently appear, seem about this period to have gone over to Christianity almost *en masse*, though the destruction of the Temple can have had no very great effect upon them, as their abhorrence of sacrifice excluded them from its worship[1].

On the Christians the same event had a double influence—a narrower and local as well as a broader and more catholic effect. The Church of Jerusalem, consisting entirely of Christians Jewish-born and observing the Jewish law, withdrew at the time of the war to Pella, one of the ten towns (Decapolis) on the east side of the Jordan and inhabited by Gentiles, but returned after the siege and founded a Jewish Christian Church on the ruins of Jerusalem, with Symeon, a relative of Christ's, at its head[2]. It is not the case, as Rothe supposes, that the mass of the Jewish Christians, bent under the divine judgment on Judaism, henceforth gave up their contention for the continued observance of the law, while those who did not do so sank to the position of heretics. Jewish Christianity, in both the kinds of it we have already seen, is to be met with frequently in the second century and not excluded from the Church[3]; while members of their community seem, in the dispersion, to have been brought into contact with the Essenes and thus to have added another to the Jewish Christian sects[4].

But for the leading spirits of the Church—for those who followed in the lines of the older apostles as well as for the

[1] Cf. Graetz, IV. 11, 78, 102.
[2] Gieseler, *K. G.*, § 32.
[3] See for example, Justin Martyr, *Dial.*, c. 46.
[4] Cf. Ritschl, pp. 249 f.

adherents of St Paul—the destruction of the Temple had a wider and deeper significance. They saw in it not only the confirmation of the prophecy of Christ[1], but an earnest of the fact that the Jewish ritual and religion had been consummated in His death. Not only is this, as has been already shewn, the burden of the Epistle to the Hebrews, but the writings of the Apostolic Fathers, too, direct attention not to the outward observances of Judaism but to the now realized spiritual truths of which these were the external signs. And when Baur speaks of the Hebrews as Jewish Christian[2], and Schwegler[3] applies the same designation to such works as the Epistle of Barnabas, the Ignatian Epistles, and even the writings of Justin Martyr, they must be understood as using the word 'Jewish Christian' in another than its technical sense as already defined. These early writers by no means contended for the continuance of the Christian Church in the old Jewish ritual. The 'Shepherd' of Hermas, which is one of the works claimed by Baur for Jewish Christianity, makes no mention of circumcision, Sabbath or feast day[4], while Justin Martyr clearly says, "we live not after the law, nor are circumcised, nor keep Sabbaths[5]." They regarded Judaism as completed and as having passed over into Christianity in a spiritualized form. The discussion of the relation of Judaism to Christianity was a common feature of almost all early Christian documents both within the canon and after its close, and, although their authors may have taken up different lines of argument, the canonical and patristic writings all looked on Judaism as a system which needed to be interpreted on account of its connection

[1] Cf. Justin, *Dial.*, c. 40.
[2] Baur, *K. G.*, p. 109.
[3] *Nachap. Zeitalter*, I. 189; cf. Baur, *K. G.*, pp. 136 ff.
[4] Cf. Baur, *K. G.*, pp. 134 f.
[5] *Dial.* c. 10; cf. cc. 11, 29.

with Christianity, but which had no longer a legitimate existence of its own.

This tendency was common to members of the Christian Church whether Jews or Gentiles by birth. The real Jewish Christians of the post-apostolic age were those who either, like the original apostles, continued to observe the Jewish rites themselves, or, like the opponents of St Paul, demanded that they should be performed by others as well. And the history of this age shews how, at the same time as these Jewish Christians were gradually becoming separated from the Christian Church as heretics, they were also cut off both from the main body of the Jewish people, and from the main lines of their development, coming into closer connection and union only with the excrescences from Jewish life, and thus getting fixed into the position of sects.

The authorities on which we have to depend in tracing their relation to Judaism are the extant works emanating from members of the Jewish Christian sects, such as the 'Testaments of the Twelve Patriarchs' and the 'Pseudo-Clementine Homilies' and 'Recognitions'[1] along with any other fragments that have been preserved; secondly, the accounts of Justin, Irenaeus, Origen, and Hippolytus—the last of whom draws chiefly from Irenaeus—and of later writers, such as Eusebius, Epiphanius, and Jerome; and, thirdly, the Jewish records, which both supply information as to the external historical connection between the Jewish Christian sects of Palestine on the one hand and the Jewish people on the other, and also shew the points on which early Jewish authors thought it necessary to attack the new Christian faith.

---

[1] The *Homilies* date from the middle or latter half of the second century; the *Recog.* are not much earlier than the middle of the third century.—J. B. Lightfoot, *Galatians*, p. 327—9.

It cannot be said that the external relation between Jewish Christians and Judaism in this period bears any very close correspondence to the internal or doctrinal attitude in which they stood to one another. The non-Christian Jews were still the vast, as they were the increasing, majority of the ancient people. To them too belonged the leadership in any semblance of political existence they still had and in the common life of the nation; and thus, in the outward relation between them and the Jewish Christians, they took the initiative, the latter being for the most part passive subjects who did not wish to break with the mass of their brethren. Now, to the Jewish eye, the distinctions between the various parties of the Jewish Christians of Palestine were of no great consequence. The latter were all Jews by birth, as well as by obedience to the law; and they all had adopted a belief as to Jesus of Nazareth being the Messiah, which seemed to the orthodox Jew to contradict true Judaism. Thus they all came under the same common designation of *Minîm* or heretics, since their doctrines were inconsistent with, though they arose out of, their Jewish creed.

But from the point of view of the Jewish Christians the case was different. Their aim was to maintain their Jewish customs along with their Christian faith, and to obtain a speculative view of the world and a practical attitude in which the two should be harmonized. And thus, according to their conception of things, they split up into various parties differing from one another in their inner or theological relation to Judaism and to Christianity.

And yet, though the external and the internal relations of the Jewish Christians to Judaism cannot be said to correspond with any exactness to one another in the course of their development, they are similar in result; and, by the end of the second century, all historical or real connection seems to have been broken off, as well as a complete doctrinal divergence to have been brought about, between the two parties. In relation to Judaism, as well as in relation to Christianity, the Jewish Christians became completely sectarianized.

In the remaining part of this dissertation, I shall trace first the external relations between the Jewish Christians generally and Judaism, and then the doctrinal attitude which the different sects bore to it, without going into details which the comparative absence of controversy in this part of the subject seems to render unnecessary.

1. A start does not need to be made here, as was done in the apostolic age, with a state in which the relation of the Jewish Christians to Judaism was almost completely indeterminate, and the germs of difference were only beginning to appear above the surface. There may still, indeed, have been some traces of this original unseparatedness among the adherents of Judaism and of Christianity in Palestine. When a new creed is struggling with an old one it is always the case that members of the same family and district are separated in their leanings, while some individuals half incline to the new faith and yet will scarce let go the old. Much more is this the case when the new religion is no foreign importation, but itself sprung out of the old, appealing very much to the same feelings and ideas as well as to the same people. But that the adherents of the two creeds were even towards the beginning of this period already out of sympathy, if not entirely out of external relation, with one another, is shewn by the poverty of the instances adduced by Graetz[1] to prove the close connection in which they still stood.

[1] *Gesch. d. Juden*, IV. 47 f., 89.

The fact that a Jew suffering from the bite of a serpent may have thought of getting a Jewish Christian to cure him by the efficacious name of Jesus[1] is by no means to be wondered at in the circumstances, and does not shew a close relation between Jews and Jewish Christians any more than Naaman the Syrian's visit to Elisha proves that a kindly feeling existed between the worshippers of Rimmon and the servants of Jehovah. And, if another young Jew who had joined the Christian Church at Capernaum, was sent off by his guardian to Babylon to be out of harm's way, that only shews the opposition the Christians met with and the dislike with which their doctrines were regarded. The only other case brought forward by Graetz[2] is of more interest than the preceding. R. Elieser (d. 116—7), a distinguished Jew, related by marriage but a rival in doctrine to Gamaliel II, Jochanan's successor at Jamnia, persisted in directing his teaching and practice more in accordance with the system of Shammai than with that of Hillel whom the school of Jamnia followed. He thus came under the ban of the Synagogue, retired from Jamnia, and is afterwards found in Galilee, disputing on friendly terms with leaders of the Jewish Christian community there. The consequence was that "this celebrated doctor of the Mishnah was, on account of his associating with Christians, looked upon as a member of the Christian society and placed at the bar of a criminal tribunal." Elieser, however, easily satisfied the governor of Syria that he was a Jew and had no connection with the *religio illicita* of Christianity.

But, not only does this event prove what indeed we know from other sources—that even the Romans, from their external haughty point of view, could already distinguish clearly enough between Christianity and Judaism, and only that

[1] Cf. Acts iii. 6, etc.   [2] Cf. Joël, *op. cit.*, p. 33 n.

some individuals made a temporary mistake as to the attitude of one man, but the conduct of R. Elieser was in defiance of an express decree of the Synhedrin, forbidding all dealings with Jewish Christians,—a decree whose justice he afterwards acknowledged.

Already in the Patriarchate of Gamaliel II.[1]—according to Lightfoot[2] in 82 A.D.—the Synhedrin had forbidden all social intercourse as well as religious fellowship between the Jews and Jewish Christians. "I will buy with you, sell with you, talk with you, walk with you, and so following; but I will not eat with you, drink with you, nor pray with you," says the Jew in Shakespeare's *Merchant of Venice;* but, had Shylock lived in Palestine at the end of the first or in the second century A.D., he had not dared lend his gold to Antonio even for a "pound of Christian flesh." Not only was it forbidden to take meat or bread or wine from the Christians, as it had been forbidden to take them from the heathen before the destruction of Jerusalem; but no business relations were allowed between them, and the use of the Christian miraculous cures was specially prohibited. The Christian creed was, in relation to Judaism, placed below the Samaritan heresy, and even, in many respects, below heathenism, and the Christian writings were condemned with the same sentence as the heathen books of magic. "The Gospels," exclaimed R. Tarphon, a fanatical opponent of Christianity and supposed to be the original of Justin Martyr's Trypho, "and every one of the writings of the *Minîm*, deserve to be burned with all the holy divine names they contain. For Heathenism is less dangerous than the Jewish Christian sects, since it rejects the truths of Judaism from ignorance, but they both know and deny them. I would rather fly for safety into a heathen temple than into

---

[1] Cf. Graetz, IV. 103 ff., 434 f. [2] *Works,* III. 448.

a meeting house of the *Minîm*[1]." The Jewish Christians were further accused of betraying the nation to the Romans, and the Jews did not scruple to bring against them the charges of secret immorality which had originated in the impure imaginations of the heathen opponents of Christianity.

To guard the Synagogue against the entrance of members of these hated sects, a form of curse (*birchat hamminîm*) was, under the direction of Gamaliel, prepared by Samuel the Little, and introduced into the daily prayers. Graetz seems right in contending, following the testimony of Epiphanius[2], that this curse was directed, not against the Christians at large, but against the Jewish Christians only. The evidence of Justin[3] and Jerome[4] seems indeed to point to a different conclusion; but their statements are obviously looser and less exact than his. And the fact of the *birchat* being thus expressly limited shews still more plainly how deep was the hostility of the Jews to the Jewish Christians and how thorough their separation had become. Nor are we able to discover that the introduction of this formula and the explicit denunciation of the Jewish Christians by the non-Christian Jews had any striking effect upon the former. The fact seems to be that they were, for the most part, separated geographically not only from the Synagogue at Jamnia but from the chief Jewish centres to which the decision of the Synhedrin would be sent, that the alienation had already taken place, and that the chief result of the

---

[1] Graetz, IV. 103; cf. Weber, p. 148.

[2] *Adv. Haer.* 29, § 9 : τρὶς τῆς ἡμέρας ὅτε εὐχὰς ἐπιτελοῦσιν ἐν ταῖς αὐτῶν συναγωγαῖς, ἐπαρῶνται αὐτοῖς, καὶ ἀναθεματίζουσι φάσκοντες, ὅτι 'Ἐπικατάραται ὁ Θεὸς τοὺς Ναζαραίους.

[3] *Dial.*, c. 16.

[4] *In Isaiam* lii. 5 : 'Et sub nomine, ut saepe dixi, Nazarenorum, ter in die in Christianos congerunt maledicta.'

decree and curse would be in helping to stop any tendency there might be among members of the Jewish communities to go over to Christianity.

At Jerusalem, however, the two parties met and came to blows; and the martyrdom of Symeon the head of the Church there (107 A.D.) may perhaps be put down as an indirect effect of the *birchat hammînîm*. It is evident, at any rate, from the account of Hegesippus preserved by Eusebius[1], that his death was brought about by the Jews.

This was a time, Eusebius tells us[2], when a great number of converts were made from Judaism, and Symeon's prosecution was, no doubt, only one of frequent collisions between Jews and Jewish Christians at Jerusalem. It is instructive to note the tendency and ultimate result of these conflicts. If Dr Joël is right in saying[3] that, in the time of Trajan (116 A.D.), imperial permission was given to rebuild the Temple, that circumstance would bring out the difference between the national ideas of the Christian and of the non-Christian Jews. For the latter, the hopes of Judaism were buried amongst the ruins of the Temple, and could only revive with its restoration; and it is not to be wondered at if they regarded the former as unnational because they had a wider view of what the nation's destiny was. It is probable, however, as Joël asserts, that many of those who adopted the extreme Jewish Christian view, sided, in this matter, with the party to which he restricts the name of 'national.' And it was just by such testing circumstances as these that the separation of Christian from non-Christian Jews would be rendered complete, by those who were more Jewish than Christian falling back into Judaism, and those who were

---

[1] *H. E.*, III. 32.   [2] *Ibid.*, III. 35.
[3] *Blicke in die Religionsgeschichte*, pp. 14 ff.

more Christian than Jewish coming to see the difference of their own standpoint from the so-called 'national' one.

The final result of these national aspirations of the Jews is to be seen in the events that followed the rebellion of Bar Cochba. It is unnecessary to inquire here into the true cause of the treatment the Christians of Jerusalem received at the hands of that leader during his temporary success (132—4 A.D.)—whether it is true, as Justin relates, that they were tortured unless they denied Jesus and acknowledged Bar Cochba as the Messiah, or whether, as is asserted from the Jewish side[1], the persecutions to which he subjected them were the consequence of their refusal to join his army against the Romans. But, when Hadrian was finally victorious and Bar Cochba routed (135 A.D.), when even the name of Jerusalem was abolished, and the Roman colony of Aelia took its place, when the Jews were forbidden to circumcise their children, to keep the Sabbath, to study their law, to observe any of the rites of their religion, or even to come within the neighbourhood of Jerusalem, it is no wonder that the members of the Christian Church there were then at last taught by harsh experience how incongruous their position was, persecuted by the Jews for betraying them to the Romans, and by the Romans for being Jews. In a mission to Hadrian they denied their identity with their ancestral people and renounced the customs they had in common with them[2]. From this time the Church at Jerusalem was a Gentile Christian Church, and its first bishop Marcus was himself a Gentile and uncircumcised[3].

How great or how small a change this may have been to that Church we have no exact means of knowing. Its members had probably varied in sentiment and opinion

---

[1] Graetz, IV. 154 f., 457 f. [2] Graetz, IV. 183.
[3] Eus. *H. E.*, IV. 6.

though not in custom, some merely keeping the law themselves, as born Jews and unwilling to separate from their brethren, others contending for strict legal observance as obligatory upon all Christians. Nor can we tell whether, after the above events, any number of the latter agreed to sink their Jewish customs and submit to a Gentile bishop, or whether they preferred to separate themselves altogether from the community at Jerusalem. Even the orthodox non-Christian Jews of the period resolved for the time at any rate to give up the distinctive observances which rendered them obnoxious to punishment, and by the Decree of Lydda (whither the Synhedrin had migrated) determined to require from their adherents only these conditions: abstinence from idolatry, from marriage within the forbidden degrees, and from murder[1].

From this time Judaism goes along its own newly-found line of development, undisturbed by Jewish Christianity, while Jewish Christianity undisturbed by it, is found settled into its various forms according to the way in which it tried to reconcile Jewish observances with a certain belief in Christ. So little relation of any sort had it to Judaism, so little was connection between the two even conceived as possible, that, while intercourse with the heathen is expressly forbidden in the Mishnah, that work contains no ban against Jewish Christianity[2].

2. But it was not without controversy that this result was arrived at. We have already seen traces of contact between Jews and Jewish Christians, and, in notices preserved in the Targum on the one hand, and in such a work

[1] Graetz, IV. 170. The similarity of these requirements to those of Acts xv. 29 will be noticed.
[2] Graetz, IV. 238.

as Justin's 'Dialogue with Trypho' on the other, we have a record of the subjects on which their disputes turned. The points on which the Jewish Christians were distinguished from the Jews were now, as formerly, chiefly these: (1) that there was a tendency to modify their strict legal observance under the influence of the freer customs of the Gentile Christians, and (2) that there was at the same time, by a Christology more or less developed, a tendency to qualify the Jewish doctrine of the unity of God.

(1) That the same standard of observance of the whole law was not maintained by all the Jewish Christians is evident from the number of sects to be met with in the post-apostolic age, whose distinctive characteristics can for the most part be traced to their varying attitude with regard to it. From the confused and incomplete accounts that have come down to us, we can see that there were some parties which yielded it a full and strict obedience, while others adopted a mediating position as to its binding force. We read, for example, of Merists, who contented themselves with observing parts of the law; of Masboteans, who, as their name implies, were distinguished by their strict Sabbatic observance, though they may also have kept the Christian Lord's Day or Sunday; and of Genists, who seem to have had no distinctive peculiarity separating them from other Christians, except their Jewish descent[1].

Much of the confusion in the extant accounts of the Jewish Christian sects arises from the want of definite names for the different tendencies. But, since Gieseler's famous article 'On the Nazarenes and Ebionites[2],' these two parties have been generally recognized as occupying distinct positions, while Ritschl has made out a clear case

[1] Graetz, IV. 90, 433 f.
[2] Stäudlin u. Tzchirner's *Archiv für ältere u. neuere K. G.*, 1820.

for separating from them a third sect—to which also the name of 'Ebionites' is given by Epiphanius—from which sect the pseudo-Clementine Homilies evidently emanated. And these three are the sects which, both from their prominence at the time, and from their historical significance, are of most interest to us.

But we must remember that these parties were not at first so clearly marked off from one another as the accounts of the Church Fathers might naturally lead us to suppose[1], and that, for example, the differences between Nazarenes and Ebionites may not for a time have been so pronounced as to lead to an actual separation between the two sects.

The fact is that the key to the difficulty we meet with in treating of the post-apostolic age is to be found in the state of parties at the close of the apostolic age, along with the conditioning circumstances which intervened. The tendency of much recent criticism has, indeed, been quite opposed to this view, and the aim of the Tübingen school may be described as an attempt to explain the first century by the second, rather than the second through the first. But it is altogether illegitimate to import into an earlier the definite views and distinctions of a later age, though, conversely, the germs of difference found in the former must be used to explain the state of parties presented by the latter.

Now it has been shewn that before the close of the apostolic period, one party, following on the lines of the older apostles, agreed to acknowledge the Christianity of the Gentile converts upon condition (probably) that they should conform to the precepts obeyed by the Proselytes of the Gate, though they themselves kept all the observances of

---

[1] Cf. Uhlhorn, Art. 'Ebioniten' in Herzog's *Realencykl.* III. 623.

the Mosaic law; that another party—the extreme Jewish Christians—not satisfied with keeping the whole law themselves, demanded that all the Gentile converts should do the same, and even denied the apostleship of St Paul because he taught them otherwise; while a tendency has also been noticed amongst representatives of the latter both at Rome and Colosse to adopt the practices of the Essenes rather than those of the Pharisaic Jews. Corresponding to these tendencies of the apostolic age, we are able to distinguish, from the rather mixed accounts which have come down to us, three different parties, or rather sects, of Jewish Christians in the second century.

Though the names are not used with any uniformity by early writers, the first sect may be called—as, since Gieseler, historians have agreed in calling it—the Nazarenes, and the second the Ebionites, while the third may be distinguished as Essene Christians.

The term 'Nazarenes' was at first the common designation of all Christians[1]; and, when the latter name was introduced at Antioch, may still have been used by the Jews to distinguish the Palestinian followers of Jesus. It is possible, too, as Graetz asserts[2], though by no means made out, that the term 'Ebionites' had at first a similar general application, being given from the fact of the primitive Christians belonging for the most part to the poorer classes ('*ebiôn* = poor). But the earliest records contain no trace of the name, and the supposition may be entertained—since the derivations of Origen[3] and Epiphanius[4] are obviously fanciful—that it was first applied after the destruction of the Temple to those Jewish Christians who adopted the Essene manner of life, of which poverty was a prominent

---

[1] See Acts xxiv. 5, etc.
[2] *Gesch. d. Juden*, III. 249.
[3] *Contra Celsum*, II. 1.
[4] Epiph. *Haer.*, 30, § 17.

characteristic, and that it was only afterwards extended to the Pharisaic party in the Church.

One of the characteristics by which the two sects of Nazarenes and Ebionites were distinguished from each other is already pointed out by Justin[1], who, in answer to Trypho, says that those who keep the law themselves will be saved if they recognize Jesus to be Christ of God, provided they do not try to persuade the Gentiles that their salvation too depends on legal observance. The same distinction is made by Jerome (about 400 A.D.), who speaks of the 'Ebionites' as holding absolutely that the law is binding and of the 'allies of the Ebionites' as holding that its observance is obligatory on the Jews only[2], the latter party being elsewhere[3] designated Nazarenes. These and other passages in Jerome, as well as the account of Epiphanius[4], shew that the two parties—Nazarenes and Ebionites—maintained their position as to legal observance as late as the fourth or fifth century. But by the end of the second—already in Irenaeus[5] —they seem to have been excluded from the Church.

(2) Of still greater importance, however, in relation to Judaism, than their position as to the law, were the views these parties adopted as to the person and office of Christ. We have seen that, after the final destruction of the Temple and dispersion of their race, even the non-Christian Jews relaxed for a time the requirements of their ceremonial law. But they held with undiminished constancy to their national doctrine of the unity of God. This doctrine they now saw threatened by the new Christian faith; and, accordingly,

[1] *Dial.*, cc. 46—8.
[2] *In Isaiam*, i. 2.
[3] *Ibid.* viii. 11, 12: 'Nazaraei, qui ita Christum recipiunt ut observationes legis veteris non omittant.'
[4] Cf. *Haer.* 20, § 9: Ναζωραῖοι οἳ Χριστὸν ὁμολογοῦσιν Ἰησοῦν Υἱὸν Θεοῦ, πάντα δὲ κατὰ νόμον πολιτευόμενοι.
[5] *Adv. Haer.* I. 26 § 2, III. 15. § 1.

we find an attempt on their part to emphasize and enforce the positions regarded as essential to orthodox Judaism, followed, however, soon after by a modified doctrine which endeavoured to share the advantages the Christian theology gained from its intimate correspondence with the postulates of the religious life.

The latter tendency is to be found developed to an extraordinary degree in the Talmud; the former, simpler and more abstract in its theological conceptions, is the doctrine of the earlier Targum. It has to defend Jewish monotheism against the Christian faith which was regarded as merely a modified polytheism; and it does so by contending that the divine essence is an abstract unity excluding all plurality, and the divine life a transcendent existence to which all self-communication is impossible, and which has no point of connection with the world or with man. 'It is blasphemy, these authors assert, to speak of God as having a son: "He is one and not two; He is one, that is the Holy One, for of Him it is said, 'Jehovah our God is a one Jehovah;' and He is not two, for He has no companion bound to Him in His world, He has neither son nor brother." Nor has man any likeness to God; if the Scripture speaks of him as becoming like God, it is the angels of God that are meant. God remains afar off from men, His presence among them being only represented by His Shechina, and when we read in Scripture that He entered into relations with or acted upon them, "the Targum transforms the divine activity or the actual relations into something that takes place *in presence of* God[1]." Thus, although they tried to connect their views with the expressions of Scripture, these Jewish writers emphasized the divine unity and transcendence in such a way as to convert the personal God, whom

[1] Weber, p. 152.

Hebrew history had regarded as having chosen and educated their race, into an abstract figment of the understanding[1]. This abstract view was succeeded, however, by a reaction which regarded the Torah or law as the complete and absolute revelation of God. And, alongside of, but in abrupt opposition to, the theory just described, Talmud and Midrash look upon the Kingdom of God as the Kingdom of the Torah, and God Himself as a God of the Torah. It has been already pointed out how, in the Jewish state, all ecclesiastical, priestly and prophetic power and dignity had come to be vested in the *Hachāmîm* or Wise Men who were the experts in the law[2]. And as the theocracy had become a nomocracy, so, in the hands of these Jewish doctors, theology became expressly a nomism, according to which the divine nature found its full and only expression in the commands of the Jewish Torah. "God is law, say the Wise" may almost be taken as a condensed expression of their creed. But by 'law' they did not mean the ultimate order of the universe, but the complex system of precepts by which their conduct was regulated, and which had been developed out of, or added to, the 'ten words' given to Moses at Sinai. "It was with this conception that Jewish theology left the path of mere negation, filled with life its hitherto empty notion of God, and placed in the room of the divine Self another in which God revealed Himself. The Torah is the content of His life; in it His thought and will and action move[3]." But, in avoiding thus the empty abstraction of their earlier theology, the Jews fell into an anthropomorphism much more pronounced than they had

[1] The subsequent development of this tendency, confirmed and defined by the influence of the Aristotelian philosophy, is briefly characterized in the opening pages of an article on 'Jewish Mediaeval Philosophy and Spinoza' contributed by the present writer to *Mind* for July, 1880.
[2] Cf. Weber, pp. 121 ff.
[3] Weber, p. 153.

blamed in the Christian creed. And God, who was at first regarded as revealing Himself in the Torah, came to be looked upon as subordinate to it almost in the same way as men are. It is spoken of as the goal of His will and action, and He is represented as affected with grief or with joy or with anger according to the position taken up by His people or His foes with regard to it. In fine, the spirituality of God and the other life is entirely lost in a theory which descends so far as to look on it as a school for the study of the Torah, and on Him as a great and learned Rabbi[1].

But, although the historical consequence of its rejection of the Christian doctrine of God and man thus gave an anthropomorphic and Judaistic turn to the theology of the Synagogue[2], we have seen that it at first confronted what it regarded as the heresies of the Christian Jews with a rigid intellectual monotheism. It distinguished their position from that of the *Nochri* or heathen who were undoubted idolaters, and of the *Kuthi* or Samaritans who were suspected of idolatry. It acknowledged that they were originally members of the Jewish covenant, but regarded them as *Minîm* or heretics since they had given up Jewish monotheism and held—so the Talmud puts it—that "the divine powers in heaven are many[3]."

In all this there is no distinction drawn between the various Jewish Christian sects, or even between these sects and the Jews who belonged to the catholic party in the Church. Nor is there any hint of the different attitudes towards Christology they adopted. It was enough for the Jewish doctors that all of them looked upon Jesus as the Messiah, and as holding a unique position in the universe, and performing functions which distinguished Him from

[1] Weber, p. 154. [2] Cf. *ibid.*, p. 157.
[3] *Ibid.*, p. 147.

other men, and that by some at any rate He was 'made equal with God.'

And yet the most diverse views found currency among the Jewish Christian sects as to the person and office of Christ; and we find, as might be expected, that the more developed Christology goes along with the admission that the law is not absolutely binding on all Christians, while those who held to its universal validity, seem to have set less store by the work of Christ, and, at any rate, made less lofty claims for His person.

In this way—by the difference in their Christological views—Origen (185—254 A.D.) distinguishes two classes of Ebionites, some of whom, he says, though they keep the law hold that Jesus was born of a virgin—admit His supernatural character—and thus boast themselves Christians, while others regard Him as born like other men[1]. And though it is doubtful whether these two classes are the same as the Nazarenes and Ebionites, the Christology of the former sect was similar to that of Origen's διττοὶ 'Εβιωναῖοι. The belief that Christ was born of a virgin cannot, however, have been universal among the Nazarenes. The author of the 'Testaments of the Twelve Patriarchs'—a document emanating in all likelihood from this sect—holds that He was at first like other men, but that the Spirit of God descended upon Him at His baptism, working in Him both moral and intellectual perfection[2] and even making Him God[3].

---

[1] *Contra Celsum*, v. 61 : "Ἐστωσαν δέ τινες καὶ τὸν Ἰησοῦν ἀποδεχόμενοι, ὡς παρὰ τοῦτο Χριστιανοὶ εἶναι αὐχοῦντες· ἔτι δὲ καὶ κατὰ τὸν Ἰουδαίων νόμον ὡς τὰ Ἰουδαίων πλήθη βιοῦν ἐθέλοντες· οὗτοι δ' εἰσὶν οἱ διττοὶ 'Εβιωναῖοι, ἤτοι ἐκ Παρθένου ὁμολογοῦντες ὁμοίως ἡμῖν τὸν Ἰησοῦν, ἢ οὐκ οὕτω γεγεννῆσθαι, ἀλλ' ὡς τοὺς λοιποὺς ἀνθρώπους.

[2] *Test. xii. Patr*, Levi, c. 18 (p. 1068, ed. Migne) : πνεῦμα συνέσεως καὶ ἁγιασμοῦ καταπαύσει ἐπ' αὐτὸν ἐν τῷ ὕδατι. See also Juda, c. 18 (ed. Migne, p. 1084); cf. Ritschl, p. 173.

[3] *Test. xii. Patr.*, Simeon, c. 7, p. 1052, ed. Migne : 'Αναστήσει γὰρ Κύριος

Origen further tells us that the Ebionites of both sorts rejected Paul's Epistles and did not recognize his apostleship[1]—a trait also recorded of them by Irenaeus[2]. This latter statement again would be hardly correct if his διττοὶ 'Εβιωναῖοι meant the Nazarenes[3]. They did not, indeed, use Paul's Epistles—they for the most part knew no language but Hebrew[4]; but, if the 'Testaments of the Twelve Patriarchs' can be taken as representing their views, they expressed the highest reverence for his person and sympathy with his work[5].

According to Epiphanius, the Nazarenes lived on the east side of the Jordan, at Pella where "all the believers in Christ dwelt together after the destruction of Jerusalem[6]." They probably remained there after the return of the Church to Jerusalem and thus became fossilized in their then position, receiving no impulse from the forces that were at work without. Of the Christian Scriptures, they seem only to have used and only to have known (beyond a few fragments) a copy of the Gospel of Matthew in Aramaic[7], or, more probably, of what is known as the Gospel of the Hebrews,—a circumstance also recorded of the Ebionites.

As a sect the Ebionites were much more widely spread

ἐκ τοῦ Λευΐ ἀρχιερέα, καὶ ἐκ τοῦ Ἰούδα βασιλέα Θεὸν καὶ ἄνθρωπον. Οὗτος σώσει πάντα τὰ ἔθνη, καὶ τὸ γένος τῶν Ἰσραήλ.

[1] Origen, loc. cit.: Εἰσὶ γάρ τινες αἱρέσεις τὰς Παύλου ἐπιστολὰς τοῦ ἀποστόλου μὴ προσιέμεναι, ὥσπερ Ἐβιωναῖοι ἀμφότεροι...Οὐκ ἂν οὖν οἱ μὴ χρώμενοι τῷ Ἀποστόλῳ, ὡς μακαρίῳ τινὶ καὶ σοφῷ λέγοιεν τό.

[2] Adv. Haer., I. 26.
[3] Cf. Lightfoot, Galatians, p. 317, n. 3.
[4] Ritschl, p. 152.
[5] Test. xii. Patr., Benj. c. 11: Ἀναστήσει ἐκ τοῦ σπέρματός μου ἐν ὑστέροις καιροῖς ἀγαπητὸς Κυρίου, κ.τ.λ.; cf. Ritschl, p. 177.
[6] Adv. Haer., 30, § 2.
[7] Epiph. Haer., 29, § 9.

and important than the Nazarenes. Their representatives were to be found at Rome and other large centres [1] as well as alongside the Nazarenes at Pella. They counted too even Gentiles amongst their number, whereas the membership of the other and smaller sect seems to have been restricted to persons of Jewish race and even exclusive Jewish culture. But in their Judaean residence there was probably no distinct line of separation between the two. They seem to have been together at Pella. There, at any rate, there was not likely to be any division of race or confusion of culture; and, in their common Hebrew descent and their views as to the binding force of the law, we may see the close relationship of thought and feeling which both the Nazarenes and Ebionites retained with Judaism. They were distinguished from other Jews by a certain belief in Christ, but, even on this point, they were unable to agree with the rest of the Church in their view of His person and function.

In general the Ebionites appear to have occupied the standpoint of the extreme Jewish Christians of the apostolic age—though disputes as to the divinity of Christ had not then come to the front—, while the Nazarenes kept more closely to the views of the original apostles. With regard to the binding force of the law the latter seem to have accepted as a fixed dogma the compromise agreed upon at the Council of Jerusalem (Acts xv.), and thus not only practically to have excluded the Gentile Christians from social intercourse with them, but to have attributed to Jewish Christians a sort of pre-eminence in the Christian Kingdom. Thus they continued to hold to what seems to have been the first idea of the apostles—the expectation

---

[1] *Ibid.*, 30, § 18; cf. Lightfoot, *Galatians*, p. 321.

that all Israel should be converted as the first fruits to the Lord, and then as a united people bring the Gentiles into the fold of the Church. But they went further than the apostles in claiming for the Jews not merely a prior right of admission to the new Kingdom, but also a higher place and office within it. The destruction of Jerusalem, however, removed any such ideas from the leading minds of the Church, and the catholic writers of the second century agree with St Paul in looking upon the Gentiles as filling the place in the covenant of God from which the Jews had fallen through unbelief[1]; while, on the other hand, the 'Testaments of the Twelve Patriarchs' still anticipate the restoration of the Jewish people, and the Ebionites, according to the account of Irenaeus, seem to have looked for the re-establishment of the Temple and its worship: "adored Jerusalem as the house of God[2]." It appears, moreover, from the passages already quoted from the 'Testaments of the Twelve Patriarchs' and from the accounts of Epiphanius and others[3], that the Nazarenes agreed in attributing, in one way or another, a divine nature to Christ, whereas the Ebionites regarded Him as 'man of men.'

Thus both the Nazarenes and the Ebionites look from the Jewish point of view, and yet manifest very different tendencies in their treatment of the relation of Judaism to Christianity. On every point the Ebionites were thorough Jews and but superficial Christians, whereas the Christianity of the Nazarenes seems to have sunk deeper than their Judaism. For the Ebionites held the eternal binding va-

[1] Cf. Ritschl, p. 172.
[2] *Adv. Haer.*, I. 26. Compare the similar views of the non-Christian Jews in the passages cited by Weber, pp. 356 ff.
[3] Cf. Epiph. *Haer.*, 29, § 6.

lidity of the law, while the Nazarenes admitted its mutability or relativity by not exacting its observances from Gentile Christians. The one looked upon Christ as a mere man (ψιλὸς ἄνθρωπος), the other recognized Him as, in some sense at any rate, divine; and the former looked for the restoration of the Temple-worship—an expectation not shared by the latter.

The Nazarenes thus broke with Pharisaic Judaism, their opposition to which is further seen in their rejection of its speculative doctrine of εἱμαρμένη or predestination; and, in trying to defend their Judaism without regarding as essential the observances laid stress on by the Pharisees, seem to have followed the notable course—so Epiphanius tells us[1]—of rejecting the Pentateuch, saying that the law was in reality different from what was generally supposed: they appealed from Mosaism to the religion of the Patriarchs. It is hardly necessary to say that the distinction of Patriarchism, Mosaism and Christianity, as three stages of religion or even three different religions, has become almost a commonplace in theology. But what is noticeable here is the identification of the first and third of these stages, and the rejection of the second as a falsification of the first: so widely did this party of Jewish Christians diverge from the old Jewish ground. This remarkable tendency is shared by the so-called 'Ebionites' (Epiphanius) or 'Essene Jewish Christians' (as Ritschl calls them), to whom we owe the pseudo-Clementine Homilies, and whose "characteristic doctrine" according to Schliemann[2] "was the distinction of the original religion from the religion of the Old Testament and the identification of the former with Christianity." It is also to be met with in Justin Martyr who, in his

[1] Epiphanius, *Adv. Haer.*, 18, § 1.
[2] *Die Clementinen*, p. 514.

'Dialogue with Trypho[1],' regards Christianity in opposition to the law of Moses as equivalent to the religion of the Patriarchs; and, as the name suggests, it is the keynote of the 'Testaments of the Twelve Patriarchs' in which the ceremonial observances of the Mosaic ritual entirely disappear, and the law of righteousness is seen to have a purely moral content.

It is difficult to say where this latter tendency may have come from, but it is not improbable that it was, partly at any rate—that is, in its view of Scripture, not in its rejection of ceremonialism—due to the influence of the Essenes, with whom the Nazarenes can hardly have failed to come into contact from the proximity of their respective abodes. Not merely the strict morality of the Nazarenes but also other traits recorded of them by Epiphanius,—such as their rejection of sacrifice and their abstinence from wine and from animal food—remind us of the practices of Essenism, while that sect was also freer in its attitude towards Scripture than either Pharisees or Sadducees, and seems to have looked not merely on its own doctrines but also on itself as of more remote antiquity than even Moses.

It is possible of course that there may be some confusion in Epiphanius's account, so many points in his description of the Nazarenes tally with the characteristics of the Essene Christians he calls Ebionites. But it is still more probable that there was a real similarity between the two sects. Essene influence would in all probability reach and affect the Nazarenes, shut out as they were from all contact with the non-Jewish world, and, by the decree of Gamaliel, from contact with orthodox Judaism itself.

Separated in this way both from Christianity and from Judaism, and gaining accretions only from the outlying reli-

[1] Cc. 19, 20.

gious parties of the latter, the Nazarenes lived on as a semi-Christian sect into the fifth century.

Similar considerations to the above may also lead us to believe that it was not a mere blunder that made Epiphanius describe a party of Essene Christians under the name of 'Ebionites.' For, while their views (so much more nearly related to Judaism than to Christianity) shut out the Pharisaic Ebionites from the Church, the *birchat hamminîm* also excluded them from the society of strict Jews. It must therefore have been hard indeed to maintain the position of a Pharisaic Ebionite, and we may well believe that many—perhaps the mass of those resident in Palestine: those in other countries might be less affected by the decree—gradually adopted the practices of the Essenes with whom they would naturally have been already brought into contact in their retirement at Pella, not far from the Essene settlement on the shores of the Dead Sea. It would be the less difficult for them to give up their Pharisaic traditions, since those into whose hands these traditions had passed denounced them openly in their synagogues; and to leave off sacrifice, since it was no longer possible for them to perform it in the only way the levitical ordinances permitted. However this may be, the so-called 'Ebionites' of Epiphanius were certainly far removed from Pharisaism, though traces of the old Pharisaic Jewish Christianity of the apostolic age may be found in their repeated references to Peter as their model and authority[1], and in their bitter attacks on Paul[2]. But their distinctive features are undoubtedly those of Essenes brought over to a certain belief in Christ,—features also to be traced in the extant work belonging to the end of the

[1] Epiphanius, *Adv. Haer.*, 30, §§ 15, 21; *Clem. Hom.* 'Ep. Pet. ad Jac.' c. 4 ad init.
[2] Ep. *Adv. Haer.*, 30, § 16: 'Ep. Pet. ad Jac. c. 2.

second century and dating from Rome, the pseudo-Clementine Homilies[1].

The relation to Essenism of the party described by Epiphanius as 'Ebionites,' to whom also we owe the pseudo-Clementine writings, has been so exhaustively discussed by Ritschl that it is scarcely possible to refer to the subject without simply repeating what has been much better said by him. Both parties had a common foundation in Judaism— in their strict observance of circumcision[2], Sabbath and the other requirements of the law. But both differed very essentially from the Judaism in the ascendant at the time, and differed from it in the same way, as well in custom as in doctrine.

Both rejected the sacrificial system of the Temple. The Essenes held it unallowable even to kill animals; these 'Ebionites' considered that sacrifice had at least been done away with by Christ[3]. And, instead of a priesthood in which one man sacrificed for the sins of the people, both Essenes and 'Ebionites' sought priestly purity for every individual. Hence their abstinence from wine and flesh, and their ablutions before food—recorded of Peter in the Clementines as well as of the Essenes—and also on other occasions. These 'Ebionites' looked upon water as having a special cleansing power and are said to have held it as a God[4]; and even to this (probably) exaggerated statement of their veneration for a material object, there is a parallel in the adoration paid by the Essenes to certain visible things as manifesting the

[1] Cf. Schwegler, *Nachap. Zeitalter*, I. 377 ff.
[2] This is however no longer required of the Gentiles in the *Ps.-Clem. Hom.*
[3] Ἦλθον καταλῦσαι τὰς θυσίας καὶ ἐὰν μὴ παύσησθε τοῦ θύειν, οὐ παύσεται ἀφ' ὑμῶν ἡ ὀργή. Ebionite Gospel in Epiphanius, *Adv. Haer.*, 30, § 16.
[4] Epiph., *Adv. Haer.*, 20, § 10. Τὸ ὕδωρ ἀντὶ Θεοῦ ἔχουσι. See *Clem. Hom.* xi. 24, and *Recog.* VI. 8; cf. Zeller, *Philosophie der Griechen*, III. ii. p. 254.

Divinity, and in their invocation of the rising sun. The dread initiatory oath too of the Essenes—though oaths were otherwise forbidden by both—passed over with but slight changes into the 'Ebionite' community of Elxai[1].

The greatest practical difference between the Essenes and these 'Ebionites' or Elkesaites was in relation to marriage, which was abjured by the one and rendered compulsory by the other[2]. But even here there is a connecting link between the two, for there was always a section of the Essenes by whom the old Jewish reverence for marriage was carried out in practice, while, on the other hand, the account of Epiphanius[3] speaks of a time when the 'Ebionites' valued virginity as highly as they afterwards did the wedded life.

The care with which the Essenes guarded the inner doctrines of their sect and the fact that a similar secrecy was practised by these 'Ebionites' make it almost impossible to compare their creeds. But both had their mystic books, and the dualistic philosophy that prevailed in the one was continued in the other. And if the 'Ebionite' distinction of the Old Testament prophets into two classes (and the rejection of one class as false), and their objections to the integrity of the Pentateuch, have nothing exactly to answer to them from the side of the Essenes, yet the latter also appear, from Philo's account[4], to have dealt with Scripture in a free allegorical fashion.

There seems to have been only one point in the system of these so-called Ebionites which cannot be traced in germ to the Essenes, and that is their Christianity. Ritschl[5] tries

---

[1] The book of Elxai or Elchasai professes to have been written in the reign of Trajan; it was brought to Rome in the beginning of the third century by missionaries of the Essene Christians.—Lightfoot, *Galatians*, pp. 324 f.

[2] Epiph. *Haer.*, 19, § 1, 30, §§ 2, 15, 18.

[3] *Ibid.*, 30, § 18.

[4] *Quod omnis probus liber est*, c.12.   [5] P. 223.

to account for this by supposing that they would be led to look upon Christ as the true prophet when they saw His predictions as to the overthrow of the Temple fulfilled. However this may be, it is just here that the members of the sect differed most among one another. For while a considerable uniformity of opinion seems to have existed among them on other topics, they held the most diverse views as to the person of Christ. By some He was regarded as the son of Joseph, by others as an archangel, while some held that the Christ had been several times incarnate, first of all in Adam and last in Jesus. In these and other such expressions[1] we see the traces of that incipient Gnosticism, which, with its often fantastic medley of Greek and Oriental conceptions applied to Christ and Christianity, was already beginning to find its way into the Church. And even here we must note that the origin of Essenism too has been referred by some to that school of Greek philosophy which has most in common with Oriental ideas—Pythagoreanism[2]—, and by others directly to Oriental sources[3]. Whether either Dr Zeller's theory on the one hand, or that of Hilgenfeld and Bishop Lightfoot on the other, can be made out historically does not concern us here. For it is obvious that, whether influenced or not by this type of thought in their rise, the Essenes betrayed plainly enough a similar tendency in some of their doctrines, and were thus eminently capable of assimilating it whenever it came in contact with them[4]. And thus it

---

[1] Cf. *Clem. Hom.*, xvii. 10, etc.

[2] Zeller, *Phil. d. Griechen*, III. ii. pp. 279 ff.

[3] Hilgenfeld, *Zeitschrift für wissenschaftliche Theologie*, x. (1867), pp. 97 ff., xi. (1868), pp. 343 ff. Lightfoot, *Colossians*, pp. 386 ff.; cf. 83 ff.

[4] Schliemann (*Die Clementinen*, pp. 505 ff.) distinguishes these 'Ebionites' into two classes—common and Gnostic—according as they were not or were under the influence of this kind of speculation (the Clementine Homilies belonging of course to the latter class).

happens that, even in those ways of regarding Christ just mentioned, we may, as Ritschl[1] has pointed out, see the formative influence of Essenism in moulding the conception of Christ received from without. A similar influence may also be traced in the extraordinary figurative representation of Christ which forms the basis of the Vision of Elxai[2]—a conception similar to that of the 'Adam Kadmon' or first emanation from the primal *En-sōph*, which played so remarkable a part in the Neoplatonic literature of mediaeval Judaism.

When we consider then that the 'Ebionites' of Epiphanius and the pseudo-Clementine writings differ from the Essenes of Philo and Josephus in no essential respect except in their recognition of Christ, when we remember that we have no historical information of the existence of the Essenes after the destruction of Jerusalem, or of that of these 'Ebionites' before it; seeing, moreover, that the 'Ebionites' suddenly rise to view from the very places in the proximity of which the Essenes were to be met with, as well as at the very time at which the latter disappeared from history; and when the only differentiating factor between the two—the introduction of Christ into their doctrines—is accounted for by the introduction of Christians into their neighbourhood, it is scarcely possible to resist the conclusion that these 'Ebionites' were simply Essenes converted to a form of Christianity, and mixed with a considerable number of Jewish Christians, who infused into the sect that intense hatred for Paul and that unqualified reverence for the authority of Peter which are so conspicuous alike in the account of Epiphanius and in the pseudo-Clementine writings.

But, while a large number of the Jewish Christians thus became associated and identified with a Jewish sect, the

[1] Pp. 211 ff. [2] Epiph., *Adv. Haer.*, 30, § 17.

members of this sect had always lived outside the main currents of Jewish life and history, and, in adopting as they now did a certain form of Christianity, lost any remnants of outward connection with Judaism they may have had before, and even in their doctrines, fell back on what they considered to be an earlier and purer legislation than that of Moses. What has been found to be true of the Nazarenes and Pharisaic Ebionites is also true of these Essene Jewish Christians. In the course of the second century the various parties of so-called Jewish Christianity became as completely sectarianized in relation to Judaism as they were in relation to Christianity,—excluded from the Synagogue even before their separation from the Church.

The course this essay has traversed shews how misleading it is to look with Baur on the early history of Christianity as ruled by the conflict of two parties standing over against one another in abrupt opposition, and by their attempts at reconciliation. What we have really had to do with was the development of a single force, which got possession of the minds of the early disciples, which modified and in turn was moulded by its environment, and which found its realization in the Christian Church. We have seen that not one of the apostles merely, but all the apostles, were impressed with this new idea, and that it led them by a necessary process beyond the Judaism in the midst of which they had been brought up and it had had its origin. Here, as always, there was a conflict indeed between the new and the old. For the customs and ceremonies which had grown up alongside of the Jewish faith in an earlier stage were not at once given up when it reached its consummation at a higher point. The old ceremonies were indeed broken through by the new step the national life had taken, and the old customs fell away. But they were broken as the bud breaks before the blossom; they fell as the blossom itself falls before the advancing fruit. The whole development was a natural and consecutive one in which the Christian Church worked out into fuller realization the idea that had been latent in it from the first, and gave birth to institutions organically connected with its own life to replace the antiquated law and ritual of Judaism.

It is from this point that we are able to see the harmony of the results arrived at in the discussion of the apostolic age with those reached in considering the controversies and parties of the post-apostolic age. It might seem at first that the former indeed presented us with a natural movement of history, whereas, in the latter, we had nothing before us but a confused medley of sects. And this is so far true. For, in the one period, we had to trace the process by which the early Christians were gradually separated from Judaism, in the other we had to deal with the relation to the old doctrine and ceremonial of those who tried to retain them along with the new faith. In the former we saw the Church led step by step beyond the circle and influence of the Jewish institutions, while those who, by their attachment to Judaism proving too strong for their Christianity, or by their narrowness of vision, could not be induced to make this advance, were left behind in the march of history, and gave rise to the so-called Jewish Christianity of the second century. It is thus a verification of the conclusions arrived at in the study of the one period, when we find that the Jewish Christian sects of the other were without any principle of life enabling them by activity or by influence to justify their existence. We have seen that some of them tried to maintain the strict Pharisaic position, and some to modify its demands, while others adopted the customs and doctrines of the Essenes. But, in the various attitudes they took up to the Jewish law and creed, we have found that they were at one at any rate in this—that they lost all part in the new development of their nation. Left behind in the advance of the Church, their Christianity was only sufficient to cut them off from the sympathy and fellowship of the Synagogue.

It is one of Baur's most suggestive remarks, that it was the same deep insight into the true nature of Christianity which made St Paul first its bitter opponent and then its boldest champion against the trammels of the law. He saw from the beginning how impossible it was for its spiritual content to be held by the forms of Judaism; and the history of Jewish Christianity is the most striking testimony to the wisdom of the course he followed. The apostolic age has shewn us that the belief of the early disciples contained an element which forced them to break through the bonds of Jewish custom and nationality; and we have seen how those who, in the post-apostolic age, strove to retain the latter along with the former, were, in their attempt to do so, separated from Christianity without being kept in any living relationship to Judaism. No stronger confirmation could be given to the truth of the view that the new religion so surpassed and transcended the system in which it originated as to make Jewish Christianity almost a contradiction in terms.

March 1881.

A CLASSIFIED LIST

OF

EDUCATIONAL WORKS

PUBLISHED BY

GEORGE BELL & SONS.

Full Catalogues will be sent post free on application.

BIBLIOTHECA CLASSICA.
A Series of Greek and Latin Authors, with English Notes, edited by eminent Scholars. 8vo.

Æschylus. By F. A. Paley, M.A. 18s.
Cicero's Orations. By G. Long, M.A. 4 vols. 16s., 14s., 16s., 18s.
Demosthenes. By R. Whiston, M.A. 2 vols. 16s. each.
Euripides. By F. A. Paley, M.A. 3 vols. 16s. each.
Homer. By F. A. Paley, M.A. Vol. I. 12s.; Vol. II. 14s.
Herodotus. By Rev. J. W. Blakesley, B.D. 2 vols. 32s.
Hesiod. By F. A. Paley, M.A. 10s. 6d.
Horace. By Rev. A. J. Macleane, M.A. 18s.
Juvenal and Persius. By Rev. A. J. Macleane, M.A. 12s.
Plato. By W. H. Thompson, D.D. 2 vols. 7s. 6d. each.
Sophocles. Vol. I. By Rev. F. H. Blaydes, M.A. 18s.
—— Vol. II. Philoctetes. Electra. Ajax and Trachiniæ. By F. A. Paley, M.A. 12s.
Tacitus: The Annals. By the Rev. P. Frost. 15s.
Terence. By E. St. J. Parry, M.A. 18s.
Virgil. By J. Conington, M.A. 3 vols. 12s., 14s., 14s.
An Atlas of Classical Geography; Twenty-four Maps. By W. Hughes and George Long, M.A. New edition, with coloured outlines. Imperial 8vo. 12s. 6d.

Uniform with above.

A Complete Latin Grammar. By J. W. Donaldson, D.D. 3rd Edition. 14s.

GRAMMAR-SCHOOL CLASSICS.
A Series of Greek and Latin Authors, with English Notes. Fcap. 8vo.

Cæsar: De Bello Gallico. By George Long, M.A. 5s. 6d.
—— Books I.-III. For Junior Classes. By G. Long, M.A. 2s. 6d.
Catullus, Tibullus, and Propertius. Selected Poems. With Life. By Rev. A H. Wratislaw. 3s. 6d.

Cicero: De Senectute, De Amicitia, and Select Epistles. By George Long, M.A. 4s. 6d.
Cornelius Nepos. By Rev. J. F. Macmichael. 2s. 6d.
Homer: Iliad. Books I.-XII. By F. A. Paley, M.A. 6s. 6d.
Horace. With Life. By A. J. Macleane, M.A. 6s. 6d. [In 2 parts. 3s. 6d. each.]
Juvenal: Sixteen Satires. By H. Prior, M.A. 4s. 6d.
Martial: Select Epigrams. With Life. By F. A. Paley, M.A. 6s. 6d.
Ovid: the Fasti. By F. A. Paley, M.A. 5s.
Sallust: Catilina and Jugurtha. With Life. By G. Long, M.A. 5s.
Tacitus: Germania and Agricola. By Rev. P. Frost. 3s. 6d.
Virgil: Bucolics, Georgics, and Æneid, Books I.-IV. Abridged from Professor Conington's Edition. 5s. 6d.
(The Bucolics and Georgics in one volume. 3s.)
—— Æneid, Books V.-XII. Abridged from Professor Conington's Edition. 5s. 6d.
Xenophon: The Anabasis. With Life. By Rev. J. F. Macmichael. 5s.
—— The Cyropædia. By G. M. Gorham, M.A. 6s.
—— Memorabilia. By Percival Frost, M.A. 4s. 6d.
A Grammar-School Atlas of Classical Geography, containing Ten selected Maps. Imperial 8vo. 5s.

Uniform with the Series.
The New Testament, in Greek. With English Notes, &c. By Rev. J. F. Macmichael. 7s. 6d.

CAMBRIDGE GREEK AND LATIN TEXTS.

Æschylus. By F. A. Paley, M.A. 3s.
Cæsar: De Bello Gallico. By G. Long, M.A. 2s.
Cicero: De Senectute et de Amicitia, et Epistolæ Selectæ. By G. Long, M.A. 1s. 6d.
Ciceronis Orationes. Vol. I. (in Verrem.) By G. Long, M.A. 3s. 6d.
Euripides. By F. A. Paley, M.A. 3 vols. 3s. 6d. each.
Herodotus. By J. G. Blakesley, B.D. 2 vols. 7s.
Homeri Ilias. I.-XII. By F. A. Paley, M.A. 2s. 6d.
Horatius. By A. J. Macleane, M.A. 2s. 6d.
Juvenal et Persius. By A. J. Macleane, M.A. 1s. 6d.
Lucretius. By H. A. J. Munro, M.A. 2s. 6d.
Sallusti Crispi Catilina et Jugurtha. By G. Long, M.A. 1s. 6d.
Sophocles. By F. A. Paley, M.A. [*In the press.*
Terenti Comœdiæ. By W. Wagner, Ph.D. 3s.
Thucydides. By J. G. Donaldson, D.D. 2 vols. 7s.
Virgilius. By J. Conington, M.A. 3s. 6d.
Xenophontis Expeditio Cyri. By J. F. Macmichael, B.A. 2s. 6d.
Novum Testamentum Græcum. By F. H. Scrivener, M.A. 4s. 6d. An edition with wide margin for notes, half bound, 12s.

CAMBRIDGE TEXTS WITH NOTES.

A Selection of the most usually read of the Greek and Latin Authors, Annotated for Schools. Fcap. 8vo. 1s. 6d. each.

Euripides. Alcestis.—Medea.—Hippolytus.—Hecuba.—Bacchæ. Ion.—Orestes.—Phoenissæ. By F. A. Paley, M.A.

Æschylus. Prometheus Vinctus.—Septem contra Thebas.—Agamemnon.—Persæ.—Eumenides. By F. A. Paley, M.A.

Sophocles. Œdipus Tyrannus. By F. A. Paley, M.A. [*In the press.*

Homer. Iliad. Book I. By F. A. Paley, M.A.

Cicero's De Senectute—De Amicitia and Epistolæ Selectæ. By G. Long, M.A.

Ovid. Selections. By A. J. Macleane, M.A.

Others in preparation.

PUBLIC SCHOOL SERIES.

A Series of Classical Texts, annotated by well-known Scholars. Cr. 8vo.

Aristophanes. The Peace. By F. A. Paley, M.A. 4s. 6d.
—— The Acharnians. By F. A. Paley, M.A. 4s. 6d.
—— The Frogs. By F. A. Paley, M.A. 4s. 6d.
Cicero. The Letters to Atticus. Bk. I. By A. Pretor, M.A. 4s. 6d.
Demosthenes de Falsa Legatione. By R. Shilleto, M.A. 6s.
—— The Law of Leptines. By B. W. Beatson, M.A. 3s. 6d.
Plato. The Apology of Socrates and Crito. By W. Wagner, Ph.D. 4th Edition. 4s. 6d.
—— The Phædo. By W. Wagner, Ph.D. 5s. 6d.
—— The Protagoras. By W. Wayte, M.A. 4s. 6d.
—— The Euthyphro. By G. H. Wells. 3s.
—— The Euthydemus. By G. H. Wells. [*In the press.*
Plautus. The Aulularia. By W. Wagner, Ph.D. 2nd edition. 4s. 6d.
—— Trinummus. By W. Wagner, Ph.D. 2nd edition. 4s. 6d.
—— The Menaechmei. By W. Wagner, Ph.D. 4s. 6d.
Sophoclis Trachiniæ. By A. Pretor, M.A. 4s. 6d.
Terence. By W. Wagner, Ph.D. 10s. 6d.
Theocritus. By F. A. Paley, M.A. 4s. 6d.

Others in preparation.

CRITICAL AND ANNOTATED EDITIONS.

Ætna. By H. A. J. Munro, M.A. 3s. 6d.
Aristophanis Comœdiæ. By H. A. Holden, LL.D. 8vo. 2 vols. 23s. 6d. Plays sold separately.
—— Pax. By F. A. Paley, M.A. Fcap. 8vo. 4s. 6d.
Catullus. By H. A. J. Munro, M.A. 7s. 6d.
Corpus Poetarum Catinorum. Edited by Walker. 1 vol. 8vo. 18s.
Horace. Quinti Horatii Flacci Opera. By H. A. J. Munro, M.A. Large 8vo. 1l. 1s.
Livy. The first five Books. By J. Prendeville. 12mo. roan, 5s. Or Books I.-III. 3s. 6d. IV. and V. 3s. 6d.

Lucretius. Titi Lucretii Cari de Rerum Natura Libri Sex. With a Translation and Notes. By H. A. J. Munro, M.A. 2 vols. 8vo. Vol. I. Text. Vol. II. Translation. (Sold separately.)

Ovid. P. Ovidii Nasonis Heroides XIV. By A. Palmer, M.A. 8vo. 6s.

Propertius. Sex Aurelii Propertii Carmina. By F. A. Paley, M.A. 8vo. Cloth, 9s.

Sex. Propertii Elegiarum. Lib. IV. By A. Palmer. Fcap. 8vo. 5s.

Sophocles. The Ajax. By C. E. Palmer, M.A. 4s. 6d.

Thucydides. The History of the Peloponnesian War. By Richard Shilleto, M.A. Book I. 8vo. 6s. 6d. (Book II. *in the press*.)

LATIN AND GREEK CLASS-BOOKS.

Auxilia Latina. A Series of Progressive Latin Exercises. By M. J. B. Baddeley, M.A. Fcap. 8vo. Part I. Accidence. 1s. 6d. Part II. Second Edition, 2s. Key, 2s. 6d.

Latin Prose Lessons. By Prof. Church, M.A. 3rd Edit. Fcap. 8vo. 2s. 6d.

Latin Exercises and Grammar Papers. By T. Collins, M.A. 2nd Edition. Fcap. 8vo. 2s. 6d.

Unseen Papers in Prose and Verse. With Examination Questions. By T. Collins, M.A. Fcap. 8vo. 2s. 6d.

Analytical Latin Exercises. By C. P. Mason, B.A. 2nd Edit. 3s. 6d.

Scala Græca: a Series of Elementary Greek Exercises. By Rev. J. W. Davis, M.A., and R. W. Baddeley, M.A. 3rd Edition. Fcap. 8vo. 2s. 6d.

Greek Verse Composition. By G. Preston, M.A. Crown 8vo. 4s. 6d.

BY THE REV. P. FROST, M.A., ST. JOHN'S COLLEGE, CAMBRIDGE.

Eclogæ Latinæ; or, First Latin Reading-Book, with English Notes and a Dictionary. New Edition. Fcap. 8vo. 2s. 6d.

Materials for Latin Prose Composition. New Edition. Fcap. 8vo. 2s. 6d. Key, 4s.

A Latin Verse-Book. An Introductory Work on Hexameters and Pentameters. New Edition. Fcap. 8vo. 3s. Key, 5s.

Analecta Græca Minora, with Introductory Sentences, English Notes, and a Dictionary. New Edition. Fcap. 8vo. 3s. 6d.

Materials for Greek Prose Composition. New Edit. Fcap. 8vo. 3s. 6d. Key, 5s.

Florilegium Poeticum. Elegiac Extracts from Ovid and Tibullus. New Edition. With Notes. Fcap. 8vo. 3s.

BY THE REV. F. E. GRETTON.

A First Cheque-book for Latin Verse-makers. 1s. 6d.

A Latin Version for Masters. 2s. 6d.

Reddenda; or Passages with Parallel Hints for Translation into Latin Prose and Verse. Crown 8vo. 4s. 6d.

Reddenda Reddita (*see next page*).

BY H. A. HOLDEN, LL.D.

Foliorum Silvula. Part I. Passages for Translation into Latin Elegiac and Heroic Verse. 9th Edition. Post 8vo. 7s. 6d.

—— Part II. Select Passages for Translation into Latin Lyric and Comic Iambic Verse. 3rd Edition. Post 8vo. 5s.

—— Part III. Select Passages for Translation into Greek Verse. 3rd Edition. Post 8vo. 8s.

Folia Silvulæ, sive Eclogæ Poetarum Anglicorum in Latinum et Græcum conversæ. 8vo. Vol. I. 16s. 6d. Vol. II. 12s.

Foliorum Centuriæ. Select Passages for Translation into Latin and Greek Prose. 7th Edition. Post 8vo. 8s.

TRANSLATIONS, SELECTIONS, &c.

⁎ Many of the following books are well adapted for School Prizes.

Æschylus. Translated into English Prose by F. A. Paley, M.A. 2nd Edition. 8vo. 7s. 6d.

——— Translated into English Verse by Anna Swanwick. Post 8vo. [In the press.

——— Folio Edition, with 33 Illustrations after Flaxman. 2l. 2s.

Anthologia Græca. A Selection of Choice Greek Poetry, with Notes. By F. St. John Thackeray. 4th and Cheaper Edition. 16mo. 4s. 6d.

Anthologia Latina. A Selection of Choice Latin Poetry, from Nævius to Boëthius, with Notes. By Rev. F. St. John Thackeray. Revised and Cheaper Edition. 16mo. 4s. 6d.

Horace. The Odes and Carmen Sæculare. In English Verse by J. Conington, M.A. 8th edition. Fcap. 8vo. 5s. 6d.

——— The Satires and Epistles. In English Verse by J. Conington, M.A. 5th edition. 6s. 6d.

——— Illustrated from Antique Gems by C. W. King, M.A. The text revised with Introduction by H. A. J. Munro, M.A. Large 8vo. 1l. 1s.

Horace's Odes. Englished and Imitated by various hands. Edited by C. W. F. Cooper. Crown 8vo. 6s. 6d.

Mvsæ Etonenses, sive Carminvm Etonæ Conditorvm Delectvs. By Richard Okes. 2 vols. 8vo. 15s.

Propertius. Verse translations from Book V., with revised Latin Text. By F. A. Paley, M.A. Fcap. 8vo. 3s.

Plato. Gorgias. Translated by E. M. Cope, M.A. 8vo. 7s.

——— Philebus. Translated by F. A. Paley, M.A. Small 8vo. 4s.

——— Theætetus. Translated by F. A. Paley, M.A. Small 8vo. 4s.

——— Analysis and Index of the Dialogues. By Dr. Day. Post 8vo. 5s.

Reddenda Reddita: Passages from English Poetry, with a Latin Verse Translation. By F. E. Gretton. Crown 8vo. 6s.

Sabrinæ Corolla in hortulis Regiæ Scholæ Salopiensis contexuerunt tres viri floribus legendis. Editio tertia. 8vo. 8s. 6d.

Sertum Carthusianum Floribus trium Seculorum Contextum. By W. H. Brown. 8vo. 14s.

Theocritus. In English Verse, by C. S. Calverley, M.A. Crown 8vo. 7s. 6d.

Translations into English and Latin. By C. S. Calverley, M.A. Post 8vo. 7s. 6d.

——— By R. C. Jebb, M.A.; H. Jackson, M.A., and W. E. Currey, M.A. Crown 8vo. 8s.

——— into Greek and Latin Verse. By R. C. Jebb. 4to. cloth gilt. 10s. 6d.

Between Whiles. Translations by B. H. Kennedy. Crown 8vo. 6s.

REFERENCE VOLUMES.

A Latin Grammar. By T. H. Key, M.A. 6th Thousand. Post 8vo. 8s.

A Short Latin Grammar for Schools. By T. H. Key, M.A., F.R.S. 11th Edition. Post 8vo. 3s. 6d.

A Guide to the Choice of Classical Books. By J. B. Mayor, M.A. Revised Edition. Crown 8vo. 3s.

The Theatre of the Greeks. By J. W. Donaldson, D.D. 8th Edition. Post 8vo. 5s.

Keightley's Mythology of Greece and Italy. 4th Edition. 5s.

A Dictionary of Latin and Greek Quotations. By H. T. Riley. Post 8vo. 5s. With Index Verborum, 6s.

A History of Roman Literature. By W. S. Teuffel, Professor at the University of Tübingen. By W. Wagner, Ph.D. 2 vols. Demy 8vo. 21s.

Student's Guide to the University of Cambridge. 4th Edition revised. Fcap. 8vo. [Immediately.

CLASSICAL TABLES.

Latin Accidence. By the Rev. P. Frost, M.A. 1s.

Latin Versification. 1s.

Notabilia Quædam; or the Principal Tenses of most of the Irregular Greek Verbs and Elementary Greek, Latin, and French Construction. New edition. 1s.

Richmond Rules for the Ovidian Distich, &c. By J. Tate, M.A. 1s.

The Principles of Latin Syntax. 1s.

Greek Verbs. A Catalogue of Verbs, Irregular and Defective; their leading formations, tenses, and inflexions, with Paradigms for conjugation, Rules for formation of tenses, &c. &c. By J. S. Baird, T.C.D. 2s. 6d.

Greek Accents (Notes on). By A. Barry, D.D. New Edition. 1s.

Homeric Dialect. Its Leading Forms and Peculiarities. By J. S. Baird, T.C.D. New edition, by W. G. Rutherford. 1s.

Greek Accidence. By the Rev. P. Frost, M.A. New Edition. 1s.

CAMBRIDGE MATHEMATICAL SERIES.

Whitworth's Choice and Chance. 3rd Edition. Crown 8vo. 6s.

McDowell's Exercises on Euclid and in Modern Geometry. 2nd Edition. 6s.

Taylor's Geometry of Conics. 2nd Edition. 4s. 6d.

Aldis's Solid Geometry. 3rd Edition. 6s.

Garnett's Elementary Dynamics. 2nd Edition. 6s.

—— Heat, an Elementary Treatise. 3s. 6d.

Walton's Elementary Mechanics (Problems in). 2nd Edition. 6s.

Educational Works. 7

CAMBRIDGE SCHOOL AND COLLEGE TEXT-BOOKS.

A Series of Elementary Treatises for the use of Students in the Universities, Schools, and Candidates for the Public Examinations. Fcap. 8vo.

Arithmetic. By Rev. C. Elsee, M.A. Fcap. 8vo. 10th Edit. 3s. 6d.
Algebra. By the Rev. C. Elsee, M.A. 5th Edit. 4s.
Arithmetic. By A. Wrigley, M.A. 3s. 6d.
────── A Progressive Course of Examples. With Answers. By J. Watson, M.A. 4th Edition. 2s. 6d.
Algebra. Progressive Course of Examples. By Rev. W. F. M'Michael, M.A., and R. Prowde Smith, M.A. 3s.6d. With Answers. 4s. 6d
Plane Astronomy, An Introduction to. By P. T. Main, M.A. 3rd Edition. 4s.
Conic Sections treated Geometrically. By W. H. Besant, M.A. 3rd Edition. 4s. 6d.
Elementary Conic Sections treated Geometrically. By W. H. Besant, M.A. [*In the Press.*
Statics, Elementary. By Rev. H. Goodwin, D.D. 2nd Edit. 3s.
Hydrostatics, Elementary. By W. H. Besant, M.A. 9th Edit. 4s.
Mensuration, An Elementary Treatise on. By B. T. Moore, M.A. 6s.
Newton's Principia, The First Three Sections of, with an Appendix; and the Ninth and Eleventh Sections. By J. H. Evans, M.A. 5th Edition, by P. T. Main, M.A. 4s.
Trigonometry, Elementary. By T. P. Hudson, M.A. 3s. 6d.
Optics, Geometrical. With Answers. By W. S. Aldis, M.A. 3s. 6d.
Analytical Geometry for Schools. By T. G. Vyvyan. 3rd Edit. 4s. 6d.
Greek Testament, Companion to the. By A. C. Barrett, A.M. 3rd Edition. Fcap. 8vo. 5s.
Book of Common Prayer, An Historical and Explanatory Treatise on the. By W. G. Humphry, B.D. 5th Edition. Fcap. 8vo. 4s. 6d.
Music, Text-book of. By H. C. Banister. 8th Edit. revised. 5s.
────── Concise History of. By Rev. H. G. Bonavia Hunt, B. Mus. Oxon. 5th Edition revised. 3s. 6d.

ARITHMETIC AND ALGEBRA.
See foregoing Series.

GEOMETRY AND EUCLID.

Text-Book of Geometry. By T. S. Aldis, M.A. Small 8vo. 4s. 6d. Part I. 2s. 6d. Part II. 2s.
The Elements of Euclid. By H. J. Hose. Fcap. 8vo. 4s. 6d. Exercises separately, 1s.
────── The First Six Books, with Commentary by Dr. Lardner. 10th Edition. 8vo. 6s.
────── The First Two Books explained to Beginners. By C. P. Mason, B.A. 2nd Edition. Fcap 8vo. 2s. 6d.

The Enunciations and Figures to Euclid's Elements. By Rev.
J. Brasse, D.D. 3rd Edition. Fcap. 8vo. 1s. On Cards, in case, 5s. 6d.
Without the Figures, 6d.

Exercises on Euclid and in Modern Geometry. By J. McDowell,
B.A. Crown 8vo. 2nd Edition revised. 6s.

Geometrical Conic Sections. By W. H. Besant, M.A. 3rd Edit.
4s. 6d.

Elementary Geometrical Conic Sections. By W. H. Besant,
M.A. [In the Press.

The Geometry of Conics. By C. Taylor, M.A. 2nd Edit. 8vo.
4s. 6d.

Solutions of Geometrical Problems, proposed at St. John's
College from 1830 to 1846. By T. Gaskin, M.A. 8vo. 12s.

TRIGONOMETRY.

The Shrewsbury Trigonometry. By J. C. P. Aldous. Crown
8vo. 2s.

Elementary Trigonometry. By T. P. Hudson, M.A. 3s. 6d.

Elements of Plane and Spherical Trigonometry. By J. Hind,
M.A. 5th Edition. 12mo. 6s.

An Elementary Treatise on Mensuration. By B. T. Moore,
M.A. 5s.

ANALYTICAL GEOMETRY AND DIFFERENTIAL CALCULUS.

An Introduction to Analytical Plane Geometry. By W. P.
Turnbull, M.A. 8vo. 12s.

Problems on the Principles of Plane Co-ordinate Geometry.
By W. Walton, M.A. 8vo. 16s.

Trilinear Co-ordinates, and Modern Analytical Geometry of
Two Dimensions. By W. A. Whitworth, M.A. 8vo. 16s.

An Elementary Treatise on Solid Geometry. By W. S. Aldis,
M.A. 2nd Edition revised. 8vo. 8s.

Geometrical Illustrations of the Differential Calculus. By
M. B. Pell. 8vo. 2s. 6d.

Elementary Treatise on the Differential Calculus. By M.
O'Brien, M.A. 8vo. 10s. 6d.

Elliptic Functions, Elementary Treatise on. By A. Cayley, M.A.
Demy 8vo. 15s.

MECHANICS & NATURAL PHILOSOPHY.

Statics, Elementary. By H. Goodwin, D.D. Fcap. 8vo. 2nd
Edition. 3s.

Dynamics, A Treatise on Elementary. By W. Garnett, M.A.
2nd Edition. Crown 8vo. 6s.

Educational Works. 9

Statics and Dynamics, Problems in. By W. Walton, M.A. New Edition. Crown 8vo. 6s.

Theoretical Mechanics, Problems in. By W. Walton. 2nd Edit. revised and enlarged. Demy 8vo. 16s.

Hydrostatics. By W. H. Besant, M.A. Fcap. 8vo. 9th Edition. 4s.

Hydromechanics, A Treatise on. By W. H. Besant, M.A. 8vo. New Edition revised. 10s. 6d.

Dynamics of a Particle, A Treatise on the. By W. H. Besant, M.A. [*Preparing*.

Dynamics of a Rigid Body, Solutions of Examples on the. By W. N. Griffin, M.A. 8vo. 6s. 6d.

Motion, An Elementary Treatise on. By J. R. Lunn, M.A. 7s. 6d.

Optics, Geometrical. By W. S. Aldis, M.A. Fcap. 8vo. 3s. 6d.

Double Refraction, A Chapter on Fresnel's Theory of. By W. S. Aldis, M.A. 8vo. 2s.

Optics, An Elementary Treatise on. By Prof. Potter. Part I. 3rd Edition. 9s. 6d. Part II. 12s. 6d.

Optics, Physical; or the Nature and Properties of Light. By Prof. Potter, A.M. 6s. 6d. Part II. 7s. 6d.

Heat, An Elementary Treatise on. By W. Garnett, M.A. Crown 8vo. 2nd Edition revised. 3s. 6d.

Geometrical Optics, Figures Illustrative of. From Schelbach. By W. B. Hopkins. Folio. Plates. 10s. 6d.

Newton's Principia, The First Three Sections of, with an Appendix; and the Ninth and Eleventh Sections. By J. H. Evans, M.A. 5th Edition. Edited by P. T. Main, M.A. 4s.

Astronomy, An Introduction to Plane. By P. T. Main, M.A. Fcap. 8vo. cloth. 4s.

Astronomy, Practical and Spherical. By R. Main, M.A. 8vo. 14s.

Astronomy, Elementary Chapters on, from the 'Astronomie Physique' of Biot. By H. Goodwin, D.D. 8vo. 3s. 6d.

Pure Mathematics and Natural Philosophy, A Compendium of Facts and Formulæ in. By G. R. Smalley. Fcap. 8vo. 3s. 6d.

Elementary Course of Mathematics. By H. Goodwin, D.D. 6th Edition. 8vo. 16s.

Problems and Examples, adapted to the 'Elementary Course of Mathematics.' 3rd Edition. 8vo. 5s.

Solutions of Goodwin's Collection of Problems and Examples. By W. W. Hutt, M.A. 3rd Edition, revised and enlarged. 8vo. 9s.

Pure Mathematics, Elementary Examples in. By J. Taylor. 8vo. 7s. 6d.

Euclid, Mechanical. By the late W. Whewell, D.D. 5th Edition. 5s.

Mechanics of Construction. With numerous Examples. By S. Fenwick, F.R.A.S. 8vo. 12s.

Anti-Logarithms, Table of. By H. E. Filipowski. 3rd Edition. 8vo. 15s.

Pure and Applied Calculation, Notes on the Principles of. By Rev. J. Challis, M.A. Demy 8vo. 15s.

Physics, The Mathematical Principle of. By Rev. J. Challis, M A. Demy 8vo. 5s.

HISTORY, TOPOGRAPHY, &c.

Rome and the Campagna. By R. Burn, M.A. With 85 Engravings and 26 Maps and Plans. With Appendix. 4to. 3*l*. 3*s*.

Old Rome. A Handbook for Travellers. By R. Burn, M.A. With Maps and Plans. Demy 8vo. 10*s*. 6*d*.

Modern Europe. By Dr. T. H. Dyer. 2nd Edition, revised and continued. 5 vols. Demy 8vo. 2*l*. 12*s*. 6*d*.

The History of the Kings of Rome. By Dr. T. H. Dyer. 8vo. 16*s*.

A Plea for Livy. By Dr. T. H. Dyer. 8vo. 1*s*.

Roma Regalis. By Dr. T. H. Dyer. 8vo. 2*s*. 6*d*.

The History of Pompeii: its Buildings and Antiquities. By T. H. Dyer. 3rd Edition, brought down to 1874. Post 8vo. 7*s*. 6*d*.

Ancient Athens: its History, Topography, and Remains. By T. H. Dyer. Super-royal 8vo. Cloth. 1*l*. 5*s*.

The Decline of the Roman Republic. By G. Long. 5 vols. 8vo. 14*s*. each.

A History of England during the Early and Middle Ages. By C. H. Pearson, M.A. 2nd Edition revised and enlarged. 8vo. Vol. I. 16*s*. Vol. II. 14*s*.

Historical Maps of England. By C. H. Pearson. Folio. 2nd Edition revised. 31*s*. 6*d*.

History of England, 1800-15. By Harriet Martineau, with new and copious Index. 1 vol. 3*s*. 6*d*.

History of the Thirty Years' Peace, 1815-46. By Harriet Martineau. 4 vols. 3*s*. 6*d*. each.

A Practical Synopsis of English History. By A. Bowes. 4th Edition. 8vo. 2*s*.

Student's Text-Book of English and General History. By D. Beale. Crown 8vo. 2*s*. 6*d*.

Lives of the Queens of England. By A. Strickland. Library Edition, 8 vols. 7*s*. 6*d*. each. Cheaper Edition, 6 vols. 5*s*. each. Abridged Edition, 1 vol. 6*s*. 6*d*.

Eginhard's Life of Karl the Great (Charlemagne). Translated with Notes, by W. Glaister, M.A., B.C.L. Crown 8vo. 4*s*. 6*d*.

Outlines of Indian History. By A. W. Hughes. Small post 8vo. 3*s*. 6*d*.

The Elements of General History. By Prof. Tytler. New Edition, brought down to 1874. Small post 8vo. 3*s*. 6*d*.

ATLASES.

An Atlas of Classical Geography. 24 Maps. By W. Hughes and G. Long, M.A. New Edition. Imperial 8vo. 12*s*. 6*d*.

A Grammar-School Atlas of Classical Geography. Ten Maps selected from the above. New Edition. Imperial 8vo. 5*s*.

First Classical Maps. By the Rev. J. Tate, M.A. 3rd Edition. Imperial 8vo. 7*s*. 6*d*.

Standard Library Atlas of Classical Geography. Imp. 8vo. 7*s*. 6*d*.

PHILOLOGY.

**WEBSTER'S DICTIONARY OF THE ENGLISH LAN-
GUAGE.** Re-edited by N. Porter and C. A. Goodrich. With Dr. Mahn's
Etymology. 1 vol. 21s. With Appendices and 70 additional pages of
Illustrations, 31s. 6d.
'THE BEST PRACTICAL ENGLISH DICTIONARY EXTANT.'—*Quarterly Review*, 1873.
Prospectuses, with specimen pages, post free on application.

New Dictionary of the English Language. Combining Explanation with Etymology, and copiously illustrated by Quotations from the
best Authorities. By Dr. Richardson. New Edition, with a Supplement.
2 vols. 4to. 4l. 14s. 6d.; half russia, 5l. 15s. 6d.; russia, 6l. 12s. Supplement
separately. 4to. 12s.
An 8vo. Edit. without the Quotations, 15s.; half russia, 20s.; russia, 24s.

Supplementary English Glossary. By T. L. O. Davies. Demy 8vo.
[*In the press.*

Dictionary of Corrupted Words. By Rev. A. S. Palmer. [*In the press.*

The Elements of the English Language. By E. Adams, Ph.D.
15th Edition. Post 8vo. 4s. 6d.

Philological Essays. By T. H. Key, M.A., F.R.S. 8vo. 10s. 6d.

Language, its Origin and Development. By T. H. Key, M.A.,
F.R.S. 8vo. 14s.

Synonyms and Antonyms of the English Language. By Archdeacon Smith. 2nd Edition. Post 8vo. 5s.

Synonyms Discriminated. By Archdeacon Smith. Demy 8vo. 16s.

Bible English. By T. L. O. Davies. 5s.

The Queen's English. A Manual of Idiom and Usage. By Dean
Alford. 5th Edition. Fcap. 8vo. 5s.

Etymological Glossary of nearly **2500 English Words** derived from the Greek. By the Rev. E. J. Boyce. Fcap. 8vo. 3s. 6d.

A Syriac Grammar. By G. Phillips, D.D. 3rd Edition, enlarged.
8vo. 7s. 6d.

A Grammar of the Arabic Language. By Rev. W. J. Beau-
mont, M.A. 12mo. 7s.

Who Wrote It? A Dictionary of Common Poetical Quotations.
3rd Edition. Fcap. 8vo. 2s. 6d.

DIVINITY, MORAL PHILOSOPHY, &c.

Novum Testamentum Græcum, Textus Stephanici, 1550. By
F. H. Scrivener, A.M., LL.D. New Edition. 16mo. 4s. 6d. Also on
Writing Paper, with Wide Margin. Half-bound. 12s.

By the same Author.

Codex Bezæ Cantabrigiensis. 4to. 26s.

A Full Collation of the Codex Sinaiticus with the Received Text
of the New Testament, with Critical Introduction. 2nd Edition, revised.
Fcap. 8vo. 5s.

A Plain Introduction to the Criticism of the New Testament.
With Forty Facsimiles from Ancient Manuscripts. 2nd Edition. 8vo. 16s.

Six Lectures on the Text of the New Testament. For English
Readers. Crown 8vo. 6s.

The New Testament for English Readers. By the late H. Alford, D.D. Vol. I. Part I. 3rd Edit. 12s. Vol. I. Part II. 2nd Edit. 10s. 6d. Vol. II. Part I. 2nd Edit. 16s. Vol. II. Part II. 2nd Edit. 16s.

The Greek Testament. By the late H. Alford, D.D. Vol. I. 6th Edit. 1l. 8s. Vol. II. 6th Edit. 1l. 4s. Vol. III. 5th Edit. 18s. Vol. IV. Part I. 4th Edit. 18s. Vol. IV. Part II. 4th Edit. 14s. Vol. IV. 1l. 12s.

Companion to the Greek Testament. By A. C. Barrett, M.A. 3rd Edition. Fcap. 8vo. 5s.

Liber Apologeticus. The Apology of Tertullian, with English Notes, by H. A. Woodham, LL.D. 2nd Edition. 8vo. 8s. 6d.

The Book of Psalms. A New Translation, with Introductions, &c. By the Very Rev. J. J. Stewart Perowne, D.D. 8vo. Vol. I. 4th Edition, 18s. Vol. II. 4th Edit. 16s.

—— Abridged for Schools. 3rd Edition. Crown 8vo. 10s. 6d.

History of the Articles of Religion. By C. H. Hardwick. 3rd Edition. Post 8vo. 5s.

History of the Creeds. By J. R. Lumby, D.D. 2nd Edition. Crown 8vo. 7s. 6d.

Pearson on the Creed. Carefully printed from an early edition. With Analysis and Index by E. Walford, M.A. Post 8vo. 5s.

Doctrinal System of St. John as Evidence of the Date of his Gospel. By Rev. J. J. Lias, M.A. Crown 8vo. 6s.

An Historical and Explanatory Treatise on the Book of Common Prayer. By Rev. W. G. Humphry, B.D. 5th Edition, enlarged. Small post 8vo. 4s. 6d.

The New Table of Lessons Explained. By Rev. W. G. Humphry, B.D. Fcap. 1s. 6d.

A Commentary on the Gospels for the Sundays and other Holy Days of the Christian Year. By Rev. W. Denton, A.M. New Edition. 3 vols. 8vo. 54s. Sold separately.

Commentary on the Epistles for the Sundays and other Holy Days of the Christian Year. By Rev. W. Denton, A.M. 2 vols. 36s. Sold separately.

Commentary on the Acts. By Rev. W. Denton, A.M. Vol. I. 8vo. 18s. Vol. II. 14s.

Notes on the Catechism. By Rev. A. Barry, D.D. 5th Edit. Fcap. 2s.

Catechetical Hints and Helps. By Rev. E. J. Boyce, M.A. 3rd Edition, revised. Fcap. 2s. 6d.

Examination Papers on Religious Instruction. By Rev. E. J. Boyce. Sewed. 1s. 6d.

Church Teaching for the Church's Children. An Exposition of the Catechism. By the Rev. F. W. Harper. Sq. fcap. 2s.

The Winton Church Catechist. Questions and Answers on the Teaching of the Church Catechism. By the late Rev. J. S. B. Monsell, LL.D. 3rd Edition. Cloth, 3s.; or in Four Parts, sewed.

The Church Teacher's Manual of Christian Instruction. By Rev. M. F. Sadler. 21st Thousand. 2s. 6d.

Short Explanation of the Epistles and Gospels of the Chris- tian Year, with Questions. Royal 32mo. 2s. 6d.; calf, 4s. 6d.

Butler's Analogy of Religion; with Introduction and Index by Rev. Dr. Steere. New Edition. Fcap. 3s. 6d.

—— Three Sermons on Human Nature, and Dissertation on Virtue. By W. Whewell, D.D. 4th Edition. Fcap. 8vo. 2s. 6d.

Educational Works. 13

Lectures on the History of Moral Philosophy in England. By
W. Whewell, D.D. Crown 8vo. 8s.
Kent's Commentary on International Law. By J. T. Abdy,
LL.D. New and Cheap Edition. Crown 8vo. 10s. 6d.
A Manual of the Roman Civil Law. By G. Leapingwell, LL.D.
8vo. 12s.

FOREIGN CLASSICS.

A series for use in Schools, with English Notes, grammatical and explanatory, and renderings of difficult idiomatic expressions. Fcap. 8vo.

Schiller's Wallenstein. By Dr. A. Buchheim. New Edit. 6s. 6d.
Or the Lager and Piccolomini, 3s. 6d. Wallenstein's Tod, 3s. 6d.
——— Maid of Orleans. By Dr. W. Wagner. 3s. 6d.
——— Maria Stuart. By V. Kastner. 3s.
Goethe's Hermann and Dorothea. By E. Bell, M.A., and
E. Wölfel. 2s. 6d.
German Ballads, from Uhland, Goethe, and Schiller. By C. L.
Bielefeld. 3s. 6d.
Charles XII., par Voltaire. By L. Direy. 3rd Edition. 3s. 6d.
Aventures de Télémaque, par Fénélon. By C. J. Delille. 2nd
Edition. 4s. 6d.
Select Fables of La Fontaine. By F. E. A. Gasc. New Edition. 3s.
Picciola, by X. B. Saintine. By Dr. Dubuc. 4th Edition. 3s. 6d.

FRENCH CLASS-BOOKS.

Twenty Lessons in French. With Vocabulary, giving the Pro-
nunciation. By W. Brebner. Post 8vo. 4s.
French Grammar for Public Schools. By Rev. A. C. Clapin, M.A.
Fcap. 8vo. 7th Edit. 2s. 6d.
French Primer. By Rev. A. C. Clapin, M.A. Fcap. 8vo. 3rd Edit.
1s.
Primer of French Philology. By Rev. A. C. Clapin. Fcap. 8vo. 1s.
Le Nouveau Trésor; or, French Student's Companion. By
M. E. S. 16th Edition. Fcap. 8vo. 3s. 6d.

F. E. A. GASC'S FRENCH COURSE.

First French Book. Fcap 8vo. 76th Thousand. 1s. 6d.
Second French Book. 37th Thousand. Fcap. 8vo. 2s. 6d.
Key to First and Second French Books. Fcap. 8vo. 3s. 6d.
French Fables for Beginners, in Prose, with Index. 14th Thousand.
12mo. 2s.
Select Fables of La Fontaine. New Edition. Fcap. 8vo. 3s.
Histoires Amusantes et Instructives. With Notes. 13th Thou-
sand. Fcap. 8vo. 2s. 6d.

Practical Guide to Modern French Conversation. 12th Thousand. Fcap. 8vo. 2s. 6d.

French Poetry for the Young. With Notes. 4th Edition. Fcap. 8vo. 2s.

Materials for French Prose Composition; or, Selections from the best English Prose Writers. 15th Thousand. Fcap. 8vo. 4s. 6d. Key, 6s.

Prosateurs Contemporains. With Notes. 8vo. 6th Edition, revised. 5s.

Le Petit Compagnon; a French Talk-Book for Little Children. 10th Thousand. 16mo. 2s. 6d.

An Improved Modern Pocket Dictionary of the French and English Languages. 30th Thousand, with Additions. 16mo. Cloth. 4s. Also in 2 vols., in neat leatherette, 5s.

Modern French-English and English-French Dictionary. 2nd Edition, revised. In 1 vol. 12s. 6d. (formerly 2 vols. 25s.)

GOMBERT'S FRENCH DRAMA.

Being a Selection of the best Tragedies and Comedies of Molière, Racine, Corneille, and Voltaire. With Arguments and Notes by A. Gombert. New Edition, revised by F. E. A. Gasc. Fcap. 8vo. 1s. each; sewed, 6d.

CONTENTS.

MOLIÈRE:—Le Misanthrope. L'Avare. Le Bourgeois Gentilhomme. Le Tartuffe. Le Malade Imaginaire. Les Femmes Savantes. Les Fourberies de Scapin. Les Précieuses Ridicules. L'Ecole des Femmes. L'Ecole des Maris. Le Médecin malgré Lui.

RACINE:—Phédre. Esther. Athalie. Iphigénie. Les Plaideurs. La Thébaïde; or, Les Frères Ennemis. Andromaque. Britannicus.

P. CORNEILLE:—Le Cid. Horace. Cinna. Polyeucte.

VOLTAIRE:—Zaïre.

GERMAN CLASS-BOOKS.

Materials for German Prose Composition. By Dr Buchheim. 7th Edition Fcap. 4s. 6d. Key, 3s.

A German Grammar for Public Schools. By the Rev. A. C. Clapin and F. Holl Müller. 2nd Edition. Fcap. 2s. 6d.

Kotzebue's Der Gefangene. With Notes by Dr. W. Stromberg. 1s.

ENGLISH CLASS-BOOKS.

The Elements of the English Language. By E. Adams, Ph.D. 17th Edition. Post 8vo. 4s. 6d.

The Rudiments of English Grammar and Analysis. By E. Adams, Ph.D. New Edition. Fcap. 8vo. 2s.

By C. P. MASON, Fellow of Univ. Coll. London.

First Notions of Grammar for Young Learners. Fcap. 8vo. 8th Thousand. Cloth. 8d.

First Steps in English Grammar for Junior Classes. Demy 18mo. New Edition. 1s.

Outlines of English Grammar for the use of Junior Classes. 7th Edition. Crown 8vo. 2s.

English Grammar, including the Principles of Grammatical Analysis. 24th Edition. Crown 8vo. 3s. 6d.

A Shorter English Grammar, with copious Exercises. 8th Thousand. Crown 8vo. 3s. 6d.

English Grammar Practice, being the Exercises separately. 1s.

Edited for Middle-Class Examinations.
With Notes on the Analysis and Parsing, and Explanatory Remarks.

Milton's Paradise Lost, Book I. With Life. 3rd Edit. Post 8vo. 2s

——— Book II. With Life. 2nd Edit. Post 8vo. 2s.

——— Book III. With Life. Post 8vo. 2s.

Goldsmith's Deserted Village. With Life. Post 8vo. 1s. 6d.

Cowper's Task, Book II. With Life. Post 8vo. 2s.

Thomson's Spring. With Life. Post 8vo. 2s.

——— Winter. With Life. Post 8vo. 2s.

Practical Hints on Teaching. By Rev. J. Menet, M.A. 5th Edit. Crown 8vo. cloth, 2s. 6d. ; paper, 2s.

Test Lessons in Dictation. Paper cover, 1s. 6d.

Questions for Examinations in English Literature. By Rev. W. W. Skeat. 2s. 6d.

Drawing Copies. By P. H. Delamotte. Oblong 8vo. 12s. Sold also in parts at 1s. each.

Poetry for the School-room. New Edition. Fcap. 8vo. 1s. 6d.

Select Parables from Nature, for Use in Schools. By Mrs. A. Gatty. Fcap. 8vo. Cloth. 1s.

School Record for Young Ladies' Schools. 6d.

Geographical Text-Book; a Practical Geography. By M. E. S. 12mo. 2s.
    The Blank Maps done up separately, 4to. 2s. coloured.

A First Book of Geography. By Rev. C. A. Johns, B.A., F.L.S. &c. Illustrated. 12mo. 2s. 6d.

Loudon's (Mrs.) Entertaining Naturalist. New Edition. Revised by W. S. Dallas, F.L.S. 5s.

——— Handbook of Botany. New Edition, greatly enlarged by D. Wooster. Fcap. 2s. 6d.

The Botanist's Pocket-Book. With a copious Index. By W. R. Hayward. 2nd Edit. revised. Crown 8vo. Cloth limp. 4s. 6d.

Experimental Chemistry, founded on the Work of Dr. Stöckhardt. By C. W. Heaton. Post 8vo. 5s.

Double Entry Elucidated. By B. W. Foster. 12th Edit. 4to.

A New Manual of Book-keeping. By P. Crellin, Accountant. Crown 8vo. 3s. 6d.

16   George Bell and Sons' Educational Works.

Picture School-Books. In Simple Language, with numerous Illustrations. Royal 16mo.

School Primer. 6d.—School Reader. By J. Tilleard. 1s.—Poetry Book for Schools. 1s.—The Life of Joseph. 1s.—The Scripture Parables. By the Rev. J. E. Clarke. 1s.—The Scripture Miracles. By the Rev. J. E. Clarke. 1s.—The New Testament History. By the Rev. J. G. Wood, M.A. 1s.—The Old Testament History. By the Rev. J. G. Wood, M.A. 1s.—The Story of Bunyan's Pilgrim's Progress. 1s.—The Life of Christopher Columbus. By Sarah Crompton. 1s.—The Life of Martin Luther. By Sarah Crompton. 1s.

BOOKS FOR YOUNG READERS.
In 8 vols. Limp cloth, 6d. each.

The Cat and the Hen; Sam and his Dog Red-leg; Bob and Tom Lee; A Wreck——The New-born Lamb; Rosewood Box; Poor Fan; Wise Dog——The Three Monkeys——Story of a Cat, told by Herself——The Blind Boy; The Mute Girl; A New Tale of Babes in a Wood——The Dey and the Knight; The New Bank-note; The Royal Visit; A King's Walk on a Winter's Day——Queen Bee and Busy Bee——Gull's Crag, a Story of the Sea.

BELL'S READING-BOOKS.
FOR SCHOOLS AND PAROCHIAL LIBRARIES.

The popularity which the 'Books for Young Readers' have attained is a sufficient proof that teachers and pupils alike approve of the use of interesting stories, with a simple plot in place of the dry combination of letters and syllables, making no impression on the mind, of which elementary reading-books generally consist.

The Publishers have therefore thought it advisable to extend the application of this principle to books adapted for more advanced readers.

Now Ready. Post 8vo. Strongly bound.

Masterman Ready. By Captain Marryat, R.N. 1s. 6d.
The Settlers in Canada. By Captain Marryat, R.N. 1s. 6d.
Parables from Nature. (Selected.) By Mrs. Gatty. 1s.
Friends in Fur and Feathers. By Gwynfryn. 1s.
Robinson Crusoe. 1s. 6d.
Andersen's Danish Tales. (Selected.) By E. Bell, M.A. 1s.
Southey's Life of Nelson. (Abridged.) 1s.
Grimm's German Tales. (Selected.) By E. Bell, M.A. 1s.
Life of the Duke of Wellington, with Maps and Plans. 1s.
Marie; or, Glimpses of Life in France. By A. R. Ellis. 1s.
Poetry for Boys. By D. Monro. 1s.

Others in Preparation.

LONDON:
Printed by STRANGEWAYS & SONS, Tower Street, Upper St. Martin's Lane.

www.ingramcontent.com/pod-product-compliance
Lightning Source LLC
Chambersburg PA
CBHW021944160426
43195CB00011B/1222